HANDS UP AMERICA

A Guide to Community/Police Relation

Acknowledgements

First giving thanks to GOD and HIS Christ who allowed me to find my way back home into HIS heart. If it was NOT for the sake of the Lord (Yahweh) Thy Elohim & Yahushua, I would not be able to do HIS HOLY WILL to Love Him and Love my Neighbors and I Love myself.

My wife, Susan L. Dicks whose disabilities are deadly in Heart and Lung Failure with less than 20% lung functioning was a victim of police, courts and correction system. As a RN on 3rd shift, the police brutality on the rise then led me to write this book in 2019.

The police in Flint, Michigan raped her from 15-17 (1988-1990) Officers met her and another girlfriend on a downtown parking ramp. There, as a little girl, one Officer repeatedly raped her and she was too ashamed to tell her parents because she liked dancing. Until now, she disliked police officers after being raped by the people that are supposed to protect the people. Many Officers have mental health issues.

1
Hands Up!

Contents

Hands Up!

COMMUNITY

POLICE

RELATION

Hands Up!

Hands Up!

Introduction

The purpose of this book is to bring attention to a matter of our Criminal Justice System that is already being discussed by many organizations and private entities as well as individual power players who are working to curb, reduce and eliminate police shootings of civilians; and civilians engaging in shooting law enforcement officers.

Other forms of police, courts and correction as well as civilian misconduct in response to poor perception of other cultures and subcultures. When the police missteps in communicating fails; and the Courts failure to recognize those who cannot afford Legal Defense; and are convicted after Legal Ineffective Assistance of Counsel fail to communicate or work for their client(s).

Private Prison Correction Officers and Private Prisoner (Business Owners) use their influence and money to help keep Judges on the Bench throughout the United States who accept political campaign donations not only for re-election, but money to send the prisoner to their prison(s) within or outside of the jurisdiction.

It is believed the U.S. system Request for Proposal (RFP's) to contract with the Bureau of Prisons who pay contracts and salaries etc.

Hands Up!

Many prisoners who are convicted are unable to engage in powerful communication techniques that allow them to communicate with inmates, C.O.'s, and learn to use effective techniques of hearing/listening and speaking while exercising their weaknesses of interpersonal, intercultural, cross-cultural communication.

The U.S. criminal justice system is a system that combine Police, Courts and Corrections. Each entity job is to ensure that life and property are safe; bring those responsible for crimes to justice (Courts); and use our penal system to correct the attitude, behavior, actions, and develop skills in areas of education, information and training.

People immediately take sides based on their perception and incidents; or racial ideology that create racial animosity and incidents that they have no room for growth of human beings free or incarcerated; or ensuring that free people and convicts are both respected, but criminals must be monitored.

Personnel who treat citizens or inmates with dignity and respect; engaging in education, information on laws for awareness. Officers and members of the community must work together and learn how to communicate with one another. The strategy used in schools will reduce negative contact and good perception.

Hands Up!

Chapter 1: Poor Perception

The criminal justice system has come under recent scrutiny by way wealthy athletes; music artists; politicians and those affected by employee personnel who stole their lives or caused great bodily harm; or planted evidence to accomplish their personal agenda as the Police officer, Court Officer or Correction Officer.

Reform was not built to bring light to corruption of oppose police, courts or corrections; it is being worked on and polished because our emerging technology (DNA) is proven that policies, laws, rules or regulations, and political influence is causing the criminal justice system to go under scrutiny; but it also give us a chance to fix what is broken to correct the perception of behavior and actions of people in or outside of the Criminal Justice System.

The Criminal Justice System is made up of the Police, Courts and Corrections that serve its purpose when we are offended by criminal(s) apprehended by police. The contact or encounter with police can become professional casual at times; especially on various traffic stops involving non-pedestrian accidents; and/or simple traffic violations, i.e. Disobey Stop Sign, or Traffic Signal etc.

One reason why the perception of police. Courts and corrections should be respected is we often work with two prongs: **Reasonable Suspicion and/or Probable Cause;** the other reason is that entities like these can change one's life forever. We have this opportunity to educate, inform and train one another on how to effectively interact: citizens and police, as it is believed that the current police training is antiquated.

For example, in the Eric Garner case in New York, Eric Garner stood in front of other store fronts being rented or owned and commenced selling single cigarettes to pedestrian who smoke.

The perception is that he was not doing anything wrong and the police just arrested him because he is Black. The media can be thanked for the reason why most Americans believe Eric Garner was right when he was wrong.

He was wrong because (1) he refused commands by the initial officer to leave the area; (2) it is against the law to sale single cigarettes in almost every state; (3) Eric Garner was interrupting commerce without a license; (4) Loitering; (5) Resisting Arrest; (6) Assaulting Officer(s) but he died because he was struggling and his heart gave out due to poor health problems.

Hands Up!

Most people bombarded with protest by watchdog groups and other groups for sensible reasons as it relates to the totality of the criminal justice system. But as it relates to Mr. Eric Garner, he was practicing the method of Dual Labor Economy.

Dual Labor Economy is often practiced in the subcultures or Black communities to survive as the unemployment number for men and teenagers are dismal. Thus, the men being under pressure by the criminal justice system to support their children and morally so; some choose to create their own way of making money.

The most notorious way of making money is selling drugs. Other ways include acting as an unlicensed community and neighborhood cosmetologist, barber, auto mechanic, candy house, food house i.e. families selling hot dogs and hamburgers for far cheaper than McDonalds et.al.

The illegal practice is rarely talked about but is in effect. The practice increased during the term of the 45th President Barak Obama in the Oval Office. But it became very popular since Blacks were freed from slavery in 1865.

However, Garner refusal of police commands caused his death as he struggled with police.

Hands Up!

The actions of both parties; Garner and the officer who used the chokehold was wrong. Eric Garner could have walked away with his single cigarettes in front of a party store that sell packs of cigarettes. Garner was interfering in a business relation.

Therefore, it is imperative to develop the right perception; and understand that the times are getting worse as people are waking up to chaos and confusion in their minds as they reflect on a system that is costing tax payers trillions and convicts a free place to sleep without no resources to rehabilitate.

The prongs used to make police contact must be taught and used so that trust can be restored back into the criminal justice system. The two prongs are reasonable suspicion and probable cause. The negative perception of law enforcement, Courts and Corrections have watchdog groups raising money and issues that have plagued human beings; especially those human beings that are in poverty.

In the case of Eric Garner and Officer Pantaleo, we may never know what really occurred on scene with the NYPD officers because if one person (sworn law enforcement) reveal something that could cost that Officer's job, the person who told will be perceived as untrustworthy.

11
Hands Up!

When an Officer is known to reveal the secrets of the department and its officers, he or she will not receive timely help or attention if they are fighting with a hard-core criminal.

Nearly the entire police department will turn on that officer to the point where he or she will want to resign out of the need for protection of their lives. Therefore, if another Officer rats out any Officer, he or she will be black balled for as long as it takes; or until he or she can show that they will keep their mouth shut if an Officer randomly selects a person to kill to get his wings.

Ascertaining one's wings is a myth (sic) that involve officers who are selected to be a part of the "millionaires club" after killing a poor White human or Black human being in the field. Thereafter, the police officer receives information on Black drug dealers who pay Officers that allow drug dealers to operate with impunity selling dope and killing in Black communities.

Black Police Personnel or White Police Personnel monitors selectee until the group concur that they can trust new member. The officer can miss days and violate rules and regulations without discipline. Other officers not included but pose a threat; a blacklist is kept by Prosecutor to scrutinize the threats.

Hands Up!

Chapter 2:
Prosecutor Blacklist

A person once said that "When in Rome – act Roman." (unknown author). One of the most hidden secrets other than the police epidemic known as SUICIDE is the SECRET of the BLACKLIST kept by every prosecutor who work alongside Department of Professional Inspection or *(Internal Affairs)* to monitor police officers who are prone to trouble after various negative police/citizen contacts.

The potential interrupters or those who might have gotten close to the underground tunnel that money laundering and Judicial Deals are exchanged and favors such as money for certain cases that will depend on the NAME OF THE LAW FIRM due to MEDIA COVERAGE, and the dignity of the media to write their perspective; and openly publish an opinionated article to sway the minds of potential jurors and friends of jurors.

The **Prosecutor's Blacklist** to contain appointees; yield ideas of police chiefs; reward him by providing positive media coverage of the appointed police chief's ideas and implementations to reduce crime. The last time we checked – the system was set up to protect life. The ultimate goal of feasibly 90% of prosecutors' office "playing ball"

Hands Up!

Blacklist ensure that the Officer noted can never testify due to credibility issues.

There are a number integrity issues in context of having "no credibility of police officers who having truly committed misconduct. But there are "Integrity Issues" in our Judicial Courts from Police, Attorneys, to Prosecutors in NOT all Jurisdictions; but in too many jurisdictions.

Some methods include sacrificing people known as casualty of war(s) who are on the Backlist; or possibly a son or daughter, family and the head chief of all media sources to control "Minds of Americans" or to judge them guilty of civil/criminal mis
or innocent before the investigation is fully developed. receives his or her orders of how to print and release the initial and final version of the conviction or death of . Other signs or strategies methods include Blacklisting that involve alleged police misconduct by those police officials under scrutiny that every prosecutor who deem breaking the law(s) by Police Officers.

In cases such as Garner, instead of answering the officers' questions and moving out of the area because 911 calls were being made for him to move away from the store selling his product without a license. Garner chose to fight back and wrestle until he died (RIP); but he did not have to die if he only would have

Hands Up!

cooperated. It is believed that Garner's perception was that he had the right to sell single cigarettes in front of stores is NOT law abiding. Yet, his belief that he had to feed his family by any means necessary was carried out and he lost his life over selling "singles."

The NYPD Officer who lost his livelihood and partial pension (what he put in his pension) he was able to get. However, the department refused to allow him to retire as an Officer. His suspect resisted arrest. In some communities of color, the perception of the police is bad news and killers. This ideology is due to many variables from poor community relation skills; Post-Traumatic Stress Disorder; resisting arrest & Hands Up!

Perceived

It is perceived in the Black Communities that police officers practice Police/Community Relations (PCR) instead of Community & Police Relations in communities and neighborhoods or project housing done frequently in White Communities.

African Americans believe the agency strategy is to aim to arrest and create enough charges to imprison people of color.

Community/Police Relation philosophy is the opposite of PCR. CPR is a term familiar with saving lives. Well, in police work, CPR involve police officers engaging in effective

15

Hands Up!

communication with civilians. The strategy help resolve property disputes; Dual Labor Economy issues; verbal simple assaults that end in neighbors working out problems.

The CPR Officer develops block clubs and crime watch organizations that work to reduce crime in their area by working with the police while leading the neighbors. If necessary; police act as Social Workers; Psychologist, father, mother, brother, sister, or relative who need of care. Care can consist of alcohol rehabilitation; children being sent to live with foster of relatives instead of juvenile facilities; but rarely do police shootings or arrest as CPR is used to develop sustainability using the CPR strategy.

Hands Up!

Chapter 3
Conflict Resolution

The police want to help the citizen(s) who call for assistance. The CPR Officer would live to help build your community. Upon assisting you; please keep your hands free of cell phones as police contact is made.

It is imperative that every person in America understand that when police contact is made whether positive or negative, in 2-5 seconds, engaging in conflict with LEO's can have a consequence. The consequences can be positive or deadly based on actions of people's action in the field or on an traffic stop.

Hands Up, Don't Shoot as someone in Black Lives Matter (BLM) created as a slogan to get attention. BLM must develop a program and use the stages of growth in their own communities and neighborhoods to stop the civil war within the urban cities before attacking law enforcement officers.

In absence of calm, visibility of everyone keeping their **Hands Up** when police contact with the intent of cooperating with law enforcement officers; things will the occupants stopped be embraced. Officers usually look to work with the occupants if they are respectful, reasonable and legal when stopped or detained by police officers.

Traffic Stops

According to the Bill of Rights, even on Traffic Stops (Automobile Stops) are permittable when a driver appeared to have violated Driving Laws. For example, if Deputies walk up to your vehicle and your and say friend(s) are rolling up a "JOINT" in Florida because the State designated the State as a place where Cannabis grades can be used for those who qualify through Medical/State Certifications. *See your States Laws for clarity.* However, in Florida, if Deputies who initiated a traffic stop and found the *plain view contraband being* open as PODS or Marijuana is legal, using the product while driving is illegal. According to expectation of privacy laws **United States v Chadwick, 433 US 1 (1977)** the Supreme Court ruled for Law Enforcement Officers right to initiate a traffic stop with occupants who possess contraband.

Warrantless Search & Seizure.

If the occupants possess the contraband under American Laws, (LE) have the right to initiate search incident to arrest the occupants because the law(s) were possibly broken. Some people in states where the drug is legal known as Medical Marijuana with or without medical cards can be arrested: **United States v Chadwick, 433 US 1 (1977).**

18
Hands Up!

The Sheriff or Municipal Police Officer right to conduct a warrantless search; and search the automobile's contents as well as detain the occupants for violating the law(s) is in the right of his or her job.

Many Americans who are privy to be in a state that accept Medical Marijuana and the use of other state legal products, the Police, Courts and Corrections may be in your future if one using is driving under the influence of drugs. Having knowledge of your state laws for the purpose of avoiding CJ system is part of Hands Up; Don't Shoot in the context of conflict resolutions. Conflict resolution is conceptualized as the methods and processes involved in facilitating the peaceful ending of conflict and retribution. Committed group members attempt to resolve group conflicts by actively communicating information about their conflicting motives or ideologies to the rest of group (e.g., intentions; reasons for holding certain beliefs) and by engaging in collective negotiation.

Dimensions of resolution typically parallel the dimensions in the way conflict is processed. Cognitive resolution is the way disputants understand, view the conflict and disagreement of confrontations that are based on various beliefs, values & understandings. Emotional resolution is in the way disputants feel about a conflict, the emotional energy.

Ultimately a wide range of methods and procedures for addressing conflict exist, including negotiation, mediation, mediation-arbitration, effective communication and diplomacy to ascertain the space of peacebuilding. The ability to exercise conflict resolution strategies can transpire through education, information and training by the agency and personnel who are charged.

As the book or information pertaining to Hands Up America "Police & Community Relations" leaders within the community to reduce the Civil War within inner cities. While many candidates in Chicago's mayoral election calls for a "more patient approach, predicting warmer weather would again usher more violence into the city" said Michael Carrol reported the violence in early 2019, CNN. Conflict resolutions training must involve the community to be viable.

Chapter 4:
Misconduct or Mistake

It has been rumored and written about by the media and watch groups that Police Officers are taking money from traffic stops known confiscation. Many drug dealers have over $45,000 dollars in their car or vehicles; LEO's conducting non-random drug interdiction stops; if the police can articulate why the money was seized, he or she is right to have confiscated it.

Other offenses involve officers seeking more personal things opposed to just receiving their salaries of being paid for the position hired. The fact that various police jurisdictions do not pay their personnel enough money to care for their family without having to work a second job to make ends meet.

One scheme that is misconduct and not a mistake are cases involving attorneys paying Officers' money for not reporting to court by subpoena in civil court against their client to build their new law practice by establishing a winning reputation in court to gain more clients in need of legal assistance. Officers suspected of police misconduct with the intent to financially gain from the illegal practice places the agency under scrutiny; thus, they were fired from the agency.

Under the Color of Law to abuse the power given to them by the Executive Office in America, the powers for police to act with integrity causes other legitimate Officers to look bad as the agency is branded due to one or two misfits.

Law Enforcement Officers across the America in law enforcement must understand the difference between a mistake and misconduct. Another agency had two officers in the traffic bureau who were taking money from tow truck drivers in a scheme to collect extra money that was eventually investigated and exposed. They too lost their employment seeking greedy for gain instead of justice for all.

For example, in the criminal justice system – we are judged Innocent before being proven guilty by theory. Once a crime occurs, the media is usually on the crime scene before the police arrives. Their theory is "If it bleeds; it leads. If it's Sex; it's Next!"

We as Americans look for the GUILITY as the news media feed of poetry and drama. The most important thing about the poetry and drama is that crime is real across America. It has grown and fallen; and returned with a revenge. The story in each city is someone getting killed by an AK-47 or M-2, M-4 or other high powered weapons.

Hands Up!

within cities where high unemployment is the culprit; but the inner city Black Congressional Leaders are not aggressive enough to reduce the Civil War within cities across America

Hands Up America is a book that purport communication before death. The police are fatigue over responding to cities in a Civil War. The Criminal Justice System is over burden with inmates who return after not receiving education from Community School Resource Officers as early as childhood. Many kids do not know the difference between a misdemeanor or felony charge. Sometimes friends or family ask young teens to ride the train; or skip school for a party; develop a rebellious attitude because she or he want to do what they want to do. When that occurs, the next thing near is criminal activity because rebellion is a (Evil spirit) that desires to plague our children, adults, and institutions like our criminal justice system.

By us rebelling to fix what is broken, we fail now as our children will inherit a system that is far more dangerous and corrupt than thought to be in this era. As children are arrested at elementary, middle and high schools without ever knowing the difference of a felony or misdemeanor. Sometimes, the handcuffs are too large to go around the child's wrists.

Hands Up!

Both young and old are sitting in some cell at the time of arraignment; and the Criminal Justice System information is in the system as the person of interest is often poor and a racial minority.

By this time the people who have been apprehended by police for possibly being at the wrong place and/or wrong time with contraband hanging out or hidden; they are eventually taken through the system and consequently lodged in NYPD Rikers; or old Attica Prison in New York for years without anyone knowing the whereabouts of them.

Other incidents that can increase a person chance of being incarcerated is when the civilian is stopped and caught by police after jumping out of a moving vehicle with the excuse "I was scared." The excuse is poor and the person running only caused more charges for fleeing and eluding.

Some civilians although innocent after being stopped by police in a vehicle wanted; or for running a red light. They exit the car and raise up a cell phone to begin filming as if that is protection. Exiting the vehicle after being stopped is the worse advice anyone can offer.

Citizens need to understand that picking up cell phones in the middle of a traffic stop to prepare to upload confrontations to Face Book live is a deadly motion.

The first 0-10 second into a traffic stop is the most volatile and dangerous part of the job of being in law enforcement. Many Officers have died on a simple or routine traffic stop with occupant(s) of a vehicle as the Officer was possibly going to issue a warning or call parental guidance to intercept the matter.

Thus, it is safer for citizens to remain in their vehicles and refrain from moving around in the front or back seat as Officers' desire to return home to families like most people.
In order to keep all safe, it is better to NOT move in the vehicle; don't pick up your cell phone and began recording or texting because as the Officer arrive at the window of the passenger or driver side door may perceive that the device is a weapon. Many people may have lost their lives as they play brave and act as Counsel arguing with police in the Courts. Yet the cell phone can be viewed as a "Shiny Object" posing as a gun.

When shiny objects are observed in the darkness of night, many officers who are smart already have their weapons drawn out. Therefore, if the threat intends to move against the officers; they entered training mod of force continuum to put down the threat with deadly force.

Hands Up!

When stops are made, please – it is imperative to keep your hands above your head or on the steering wheel until you receive instructions within the 10-minute window. Citizens have lost their live as they tried to use a camera for footage on their Social Media Accounts to shame Law Enforcement by showing the public how much they know.

A leader said, "People don't care how much you know; until they know how much you care." (Gen. Swartzenkoff). Keep your hands up; and the **Police officers will most likely not shoot**.

Chapter 5:
Methodology of Catch/Release

Remember, Community/Police Relations is a spark that will propel your neighborhood to heights that other communities will want to know the secret of how to keep the crime low and away from the people in the District.

This will require dads, moms, children and grandchildren; so that the great grandchildren can forge ahead with justice in their hearts as they join the Police; Prosecutors; Judges; and Wardens as well as Correction Officers in revising the CJ System by teaching young people not to get involved with crime.

It will be their opportunity to pick up the new Criminal Justice System that is filled with Integrity and Justice for All by teaching them how much you care; and NOT how much you know. Those who offended will become one of the best community activists.

Returning to prison is high amongst African American Communities and the hope that is snuffed out after crimes are committed is used against him or her for the remainder of their lives. Thus, Blacks re-offend because no safety net is there to catch them as safety nets are laid out for poor Whites who receive Community/Police Relations.

Hands Up!

The incarceration rates in 2019 was alone in the Federal Prison 68% Blacks; 18% Whites; and 16% Latinos (CNN Poll) disparate treatment caused President Trump Reform of the Federal Guidelines & incarceration rates. The high numbers were reversed as he commuted many Federal sentences, but the News Outlets have not given him any Credit for the work he has done as the President.

In the previous system, certain Elected Officials were invested in Private Prisons as the incarceration rates skyrocketed in the 90'. Many (innocent) people were incarcerated because money was at the center of the table as schemes such **convict leasing** was introduced by **"Tricky Dick"** as President Nixon allowed **PP Owners** to begin profiting from free work done by Prisoners for $35-$45 thousand dollars.

Sheriff to PP warden or owners whose convicts were (guilty) and (innocent) convicts were being released to certain employers for labor. The money in the 1930's & 1940's was equivalent to $300,000 to $450,000 today.

The $30,000 to $50,000 which was equivalent to $200-$400,000 from the free labor from convicts that earned P.P millions. Convict Leasing would cause hostility today as the wardens and PP owners were to get exposed. The vicarious liability for the jobs and prisons would be very expensive taken into consideration liability. Insurance.

However, if we re-examine the system, Tricky Dick" was not too far from the future. We need **Convict Leasing"** but we would have to select certain non-violent prisoners to participate as well as an industry to conform to the new CJ System.

The job must not be harmful for prison workers or other lives such as employees as unqualified work may be threatened with money hungry CEO's whose product remain fractured after incarceration. Now that we are familiar with the Police, we can examine the courts as the next entity that will cause tax payor marching for justice as they are starting to do so due to the injustices that is transpiring from within the Courts.

The use of Community/Police Relations will help develop a better perception; and the methodology used under CPR should be a standard method to curb violence and reduce attitudes against police. If CPR is used and leaders are formed to protect their communities, we will have an opportunity to stop the Civil War and Genocide of African Americans who are killing one another first.

Chapter 6:
Urban Civil War

The information being transcribed as we released the statistical data of 68% Blacks, 18% White and 16% Latino is serving in the Federal Prisons. Although the President is allowing Hon. Jared Kushner reform portions of the CJ System, it is evident that before prison reform can be effective, it is imperative that the Government of the U.S. address the Urban Civil War that exist in nearly every city in America.

In nearly every city, a young boy or girl can find a handgun that was used in a crime or brand new. In some cases, the man on the street in a clandestine operation is selling high powered guns and all sorts of artillery to kill or maim human beings. The weapon of choice in almost every city is a 9mm or high-powered rifle.

The killings that we expect police to curb is a civil war in cities where people who have color are killing one another in cities across America but marching for peace and justice. A cease and desist should be sent to Governor and Mayor to advise all gangs and violent individuals that use guns to solve their financial woes must be imprisoned. In some cases, the death row must be re-instituted as cases eligible must be examined thoroughly.

Hands Up!

Historically, incarceration levels of racial indifference can be certified as valid because the author son was gun down (14) times as he was being sworn in as Chief of Police. Still, Latino and Black Americans are murdering one another for sport or territory to move drugs and guns as well as other contraband.

The CJ System with autonomy must maintain integrity. Most racial minorities are residing in ghettos that are festered with drugs and guns. The people who have resided in the community when it was economically viable are being pushed out and dying.

The descendants are left with being in a city plagued with criminals who break into homes of the elderly; one man broke into a home of a Retired Lt. Deputy Sheriff in Michigan was killed in his home after thugs broke into his home to take his life.

Thus, we need our police officers inside of the jurisdiction to help slow down the Civil War and they are left with complaints or loss of job after they work everyday inside a War Zone that may have caused the Officer PTSD Post-Traumatic Stress Disorder. The disorder is already causing the many officers to commit suicide by gun before or after retiring after working daily inside the cities in which the government will not call it Civil Wars.

Hands Up!

The Justice System encompasses all phases of the criminal justice system as individuals and groups fighting separate battles. One or more people may be fighting the Police; while the assailants against the antiquated aggression; Court injustices; and Correction Facilities that are not teaching inmates rehabilitation.

The rehabilitation can start at childhood level as each racial minority child, adolescent, adults, senior and elderly learn the difference between felony and misdemeanors. This information can be shared in elementary, middle and high schools throughout the country to help educate, inform and training on crime and punishment in schools; and community/police relations.

For example, one School Resource Officer was arresting young children whose handcuffs were too large to go around (9) school age children who were in middle school. He would always say that he was going to stop Black kids from being Officers and he is a Black Police Officer. The children who were arrested as minors became juvenile delinquents; while others were angry because they were unable to get gainful employment because of a minor status arrests effected by the School Resource Officers behavior. Effecting an arrest of minor children cause early delinquency and future War mongers.

Some people may disagree with the assessment of inner cities being inundated with 911 calls due to Civil Wars. The crimes range from minor to major crimes. The mind of law enforcement officers responding to crimes are often concerned about the safety of self and colleagues responding.

The mindset is consistent with the law and rules and regulations. But the adrenaline that runs through the veins of every cop starts with fear then bravery. In the case of Garner v NYPD, Garner died by a choke hole known to be illegal.

After 5-years after his death, politicians pressured by certain organizations coerced the City and NYPD Police Administrators to end his employment by terminating him as the lone person responsible for the death of Garner. The racial minority groups as well as some Whites as well as the Mayor of New York to demand his resignation or termination for the death of Eric Garner.

The NYPD plain clothes division initiated enforcing Eric Garner to leave for selling single cigarettes to survive. But the store owner was not allowing Garner to conduct dual labor economy practices in front of his store as a way of short-changing the owner who pay State taxes for the business he owns.

Hands Up!

When the Officer was fired by political grandstanding, it caused disruption within rank and file. Agency officers disagreed with the decision as resisting arrest is the culprit.

Politics and Police
Police/Community Relations works as it did in days of old. We now have technology and ways of communicating that can inspire people to leave the area. Politics is significant; but policing civil wars is policing.

Mr. Eric Garner who was strangled by certain or one member of the NYPD after requesting him to move off the corner per the owner.

For example, entrepreneurs who own corner stores who participate in society economy is challenged by people like Garner who sale single cigarettes as they engage in dual labor economy practices in front of the corner stores or selling food without permission from the owner or City inspectors.

The death of Garner was caused by resisting arrest and not only the choke hold. It was reported that he had serious health issues that contributed to his death as he resisted arrest although he was advised that his actions were illegal and due to resisting arrest - he died. Garner heart stopped after resisting arrest under color of law as the Civil War continues.

34
Hands Up!

Chapter 4: Academy Communication

Great police officers working day and night and going from minor incidents to major crimes like homicides, shooting, stabbings, sexual assaults, and assault with intent to do great bodily harm as well as traffic accidents without complaining is expected.

The important lesson in attending and graduating from the police academy create an opportunity to learn the criminal/civil laws of the jurisdiction in which life and property is protected. Behavior of law enforcement officers should be in accordance with those laws; as well as the rules and regulations of the Police Agency.

Moreover, every police contact involves police procedural due process in the field. Due Process includes making encounters based on reasonable suspicion or probable cause before initiating **Terry Stops or Terry Pats and arresting someone in America.**

We all must re-develop affection for police who run toward violent crimes with danger lurking as the Urban Civil Wars cause PTSD. Police Against Violence Everywhere (P.A.V.E) initiated in Flint/Genesee County Michigan by Chief David R. Dicks advocates Community & Police Relations and violence.

Communication Approach
Categories of employee training is predicated on the ability for our heroes to effectively communicate with citizens of America or Immigrants.

This chapter defines employee training, examines the role of training in onboarding programs; and administrators must develop, prepare, plan, strategize and executing programs that surround communications.

Police Model that would gain the confidence of the leaders in the community to be able to stand with the perception "If you do something in this area, the police will be here in 10-seconds" type of words around the streets.

Those who choose to work with Deputies or Inner-City Police are there to facilitate and provide statistical data (stats sheet) to break down where crime is occurring.

Also, the leaders ought to lead the Community Crime Watch meetings as the LEO's job is to collect information from group leaders have the ability report crimes as well as suspects involved in crimes.

Chapter 6: Fair Media Coverage

The purpose of American Media is to report accurate, fair and balanced news of multiple areas. The subjects such as Religion, Economics, Social Media, Politics and Police.

Each category has its own spin and sometimes misleading information that create racial, religious, economic, social media, politics and policing to gain mass coverage for awards and individual achievements that serve themselves and the organization rather than serving the people within the jurisdiction information that contribute to growth. Growth of individuals and organizations to create better human beings should be the goal.

"If it bleeds; it leads" (unknown author) ranks high on the reasons why the media report information that is misleading at times; and unfair in many instances as it relates to many of the subject(s) in which most Americans receive their knowledge of the world.

One subject that we must be conscience of is the United States Constitution and Bill of Rights of America. How to appropriately respond to police is within the framework of our U.S. Constitution – Bill of Rights.
The greatest nation on earth have rules that share with us on being fair without discriminating or reverse discrimination; but

Hands Up!

in reporting news on law enforcement officers; especially of the critical incident is a police shooting.

The media resort to "If it bleeds – it leads; if it is sex, it's next" as they select what type **tel-e-vision** and being fair in doing so. One matter that is causing bias reporting and false narratives as well as their contribution to city riots are fed to subcultural groups who already fear the police.

However, in fearing law enforcement – Black or African American Law Enforcement Officers have committed crimes or police misconduct against Black citizens feasibly more than the public sees or witness.

But when White Police Officers are involved in the same reaction essential to saving their own lives, they are demonized by a biased media who does not report the police abuse initiated and executed in the field by some Black Law Enforcement Officers where colleagues were disciplined or fired for the same offense.

The media are not interested in Black people being killed by Black Police Officers. Thus, demonizing White colleagues is unfair President Trump who support for all law enforcement officers, except those who commit crimes without thought.

The author has read and investigated as well as observed Black Police Officers provoke suspects as a Chief of Police and Rookie Cop. In both situations, there is consequences for exposing an Officer or multiple Officers involved in misconduct.

All Black Cops do NOT use poor judgement, engage in police misconduct; initiate police brutality and arrest children. But if statistics were to be collected in a non-bias sampling using both Whites and Blacks beginning in the 1970's – Present, many Black Police Officers has and are engaging in illegal activities that are NOT being reported in the same way as their colleagues of another race.

Sexual Assaults
In policing, sexual assaults are crimes that require an extensive investigation. The last thing that the citizens in jurisdictions patrolled by police; and especially the School Resource Officers were alleged to be raping school age children as school resource officers.

One case involved a 8th grader who met her lover in middle school as the Officer was good friends with the 5th Black Chief.
It was widely being reported in the streets that certain School Resource Officers were engaging in sexual relations with school age

children as they used their uniform and plain clothes and philandering ways to attract young children in middle school who admired law enforcement officers who sexually assaulted children.

In reflection, confidential informants were reporting that the Officers having advantage over children were going into the basement of the middle school and engaging in sexual relations. The young girl who became an adult with no gainful employment to support the child they had together, the Officer connection with the Chief of Police received favor from the top cop to hire his young/adult lover.

The adult female rookie graduated from the academy and the administration assigned her to the community relations division.

Some Black colleagues knew that the two were intimate while she was a teenager in middle school; but with no solid proof the information was only a rumor.

Changing Top Cops
Years had passed as field officers were accused of stealing $45,000 dollars on a traffic stop; and school officers remained.

Chapter 7:
Politics and Policing

Upon administration changing top cops, many if NOT all School Resource Officers were relieved of their positions. Many filed grievances with the union but to no avail they were assigned to patrol division.

The female rookie gained time on the force until being stalked by her childhood lover. She requested that the chief put him in check as his behavior included Domestic Violence.

As his actions of DV and Intimate Spouse Abuse elements were revealed, she felt coerced to seek gainful employment with another police agency. Prior to resigning, she informed many people on the department that she had been intimate with the school resource officer since the 8th grade to get him to leave her alone. The 3-year rookie was eventually hired by another agency.

Source Selection
When City Administrators win political contests, they select their own administrative personnel.

When one top cop who maintained integrity as an Officer son was shot on the day of his inauguration as chief. The son of the new

Hands Up!

chief was shot over 12-times by four young men from 18-20's, but only (3) were charged. Although a small fraction of police personnel was angry at the selection of chief, it was their intent to put fear in the chief by murdering his son.

The (4) Black Men who killed the chief's son to send a message through someone with interest in the chief's position sought to scare the chief into the plan to restructure the agency.

The message of murder only enraged the chief. A team was assembled by the chief himself as the men were apprehended with two-weeks after the murder.

Descendants of the Civil War
The young Black killers were apprehended as Police Detectives were quick to try to label the crime as drug related like most young black men receives after engaging murder or being murdered within the urban civil war.

The idea that (4) men engaged in killing the 24-year old male black and son of the new chief; the chief knew it was a message.

The (3) descendants of the urban civil war that law enforcement working in the field are running 911 calls and seeing bodies like the chief son nearly every day are/were affected.

Hands Up!

The chief exposure to **policing** and **politics hurt him as (3) of the killers were let go.** The disdain for the 6th African American Chief of one of the most dangerous cities in America was traumatized after the Prosecutor charged only one (1) man who was later convicted of 2nd Degree Murder.

Politics in policing is partly why Officer Pantaleo of NYPD who used a prohibited choke-hold maneuver while attempting to arrest Garner for the unlicensed sale of loose cigarettes as a dual labor economy charge is rarely practiced.

Organizations such as the media and Black organizations pressured the Mayor of New York for nearly five years after Garner stood in front of open store fronts in 2014. The City Store Front owners are feasibly constituents of the mayor as well as other Aldermen or Commissioners.

During the store front conflict as Mr. Garner resisted arrest for loitering or other local law or ordinances that prohibit i.e. an unlicensed professional to sell {single cigarette(s)} and other contraband.

Hands Up is one of the first thoughts most Americans; especially those people with disabilities would do if surrounded by multiple officers.

If Officer Pantaleo received a 911 call or reasonable suspicion to check Garner practicing dual labor employment. The fact that a violation could have been cited for Garner selling single cigarettes as mostly Indian and Arab American or Sikhs' sell single cigarettes from within the store fronts, Garner interfering in business relations could become loitering and other citations i.e., misdemeanor(s).

The media displayed Garner resisting arrest as Officer Pantaleo along with other NYPD investigators. Less likely than not they knew of Garner's health information. But as the bias media portrayed Officer Pantaleo and other White Law Enforcement Officers assisting him tame a large framed crazed African American or other struggling with investigators after being feasibly told to just leave the area.

Mr. Garner (RIP) did not cooperate with police. The only verbal language and bi-party physical aggression shown by the media repeatedly was the final physical aggressive chokehold deemed an illegal chokehold that finally caused Garner to (TAP OUT) - MMA style chokehold.

Despite the high unemployment in the City of New York under the Honorable Mayor Bill De Blasio battling the city's Black high

Hands Up!

unemployment and failed Bid for President was under political pressure to fire Pantaleo. Pantaleo and countless Black Officers use it. The politics of some Black Organizations seek to benefit financially, politically and personally by exploiting emotional pain.

It is feasibly that it was NOT Officer Pantaleo's thought that he was going to kill a black man in New York in the area of businesses. It is a fact that Officer Pantaleo heart to serve the city in War Zones and laws surpassing the Geneva Convention publicly convicted him because he is a White Officer.

The Police in Politics are taking down some of our best men in policing. It was determined after five-years, Officer Pantaleo was fired in 2019; according to the Police Commissioner he was disallowed to collect his police pension; but Pantaleo who is no longer a sworn police officer was allowed to collect was he put into his Police Retirement.

It brought tears of sadness from the eyes after learning (5) years later the city would cave into political pressure by firing a worker who is a hard charger. In an opinion, it is believed that Pantaleo went under federal and local scrutiny after the Chokehold. Due to the resisting arrest and the disrespect to society business owners, law enforcement, and society practicing a dual labor economy

45
Hands Up!

because of the high unemployment cause the Honorable Mayor Bill De Blasio to fall to political pressure and destroy Pantaleo.

lack of Will Power to walk away.

the author as the culture of police is to help and NOT to harm. to collected what he put in his pensions are demonized and their livelihood taken after defending their lives against skilled killer living and playing in the urban war zones of the cities of North America.

Making White Law Enforcement Officers or Deputies the face of racial hostility and police brutality under the Color of Law is unfair. Post-Traumatic Stress Disorder (PTSD) is causing many long-term tenured police Veterans to go Home after each critical incident and watch the latest sporting event; or drama action police show; while suffering internally because he/she were not debriefed after Critical Incident.

Debriefing is NOT something a Counselor has to do. It is something that the Chief or Sheriff must adopt or invent programs police personnel before any police officers who are fatigued commit misconduct or police suicide. that morning or afternoon or early as last week. The act of name calling shows no

46
Hands Up!

sympathy. The way to the man's or woman's heart is the truth. Be careful, that let us know if you feel funny about certain crimes so we can debrief you in dealing with the evidence. Perceptions can change when crowds faced with critical situations of family or friends can contribute to misdirected anger toward police. The perception of negative and insensitivity of law enforcement desire to help is confused with us against them mentality. The positive outlook is reduced after responding officers disrespect civilians or civilians disrespect police.

Exhaustion
Homicides and double homicides or critical incidents that require multiple police personnel to control crowds and losing critical evidence. If evidence is not to captured police exhaustion increases. Many civilians in racial minority communities often perceive the police as negative; and flee the scene (1) no parental education (2) poor music (3) no parental guide on television shows (4) subcultural opinion of police 5. friends run (7) Stolen items (8) Contraband. Every day, law enforcement with all the equipment on their bodies; numerous 911 calls needing to be responded to in minutes down to the hour per the police administration. The encountering of suspects who enjoy fighting and brutalizing the police.

Handgun, alcohol, drugs, PWID; Recent Crime Spree; Homicides and Sexual Assaults and vicious killing amongst subcultures who attack others who try to make it reduce or go away – and murder the people that look like them as far as racial ethnic relations.

Some of the leaders often find it wise to call the local news when a White Police Officer shoot down a Black Man or Teen while the incident was captured on tape; the media blows it all up to cause rioting as authorities is ordered to use money for possible riots.
The crowd of people on crime scenes usually does not lean on the side of caution as it relates to evidence is trampled over as multiple people start chanting "What do we want Justice! No Justice, No Peace!" As the groups like Black Lives Matter (BLM) prepare to dominate the news in every city to get exposure and act as if they know the full spectrum of what took place.

Much of the information inundated with the untruth and truth, more people who choose to believe that the White Police Not Black Police trampled all over the rights of people without considering their racial make-up.

Law enforcement officers can be subjected to running or driving to 75-81 (911) calls in one day depending jurisdictional areas and the complexity of the call in the inner cities. The

Deputies or Officers are working very hard to maintain law and order on the streets. In concluding this chapter, the perception of both the Police and Citizens need to be repaired as courses on Community/Police Relations his held in 6-weeks. Officers from each district will only be accountable for introducing themselves to the leaders in the community; and patrolling that area and being accountable to the leaders.

Various styles of communication is used to establish a Community/Oriented Police.

IMPACT
Given that crime breeds money, street money and corporate money; the system must be revamped to rule out poor strategies by police agencies to win the public trust. Winning the inner city public trust will make life easy. Life will be made easy when the leaders throughout the Country get on the same page surrounding Community/Police Relations.

Community/Police/Relations is significantly different from Police/Community Relations **First:** Community/Police Relations involves the Police Agency pairing up with the leaders of the Communities throughout the County but NOT crossing Jurisdictional Lines.

Community/Policing has the appearance of allowing the leaders and participants to use

Community Block Grant Funding to buy enough Community/Patrol Units that are qualified to carry a Handgun; only act in the best interest of the Department when saving a life or lives; employment & no-recidivism.

Develop a time and place of continuous training for City Volunteers known Community Patrol & Investigations (CPI). This strategy is more intelligent than it looks on paper. The program calls for background checks and mini-police academy on Rules and Regulations first; and Laws as well as Ordinances to secondly understand that Laws overrule Rules and Regulations most times.

Many cities may be already doing something similar that interest the entire Criminal Justice System. But Community/Police Relation (CPR) Model 2020 in Hands Up America will revive the inner cities because the presence of the Volunteers acting as Eyes and Ears as Retirees or Young Students who look to serve or impress employers with discipline in contributing to society under the CJ System Reform. This is the first level of volunteerism.

Many Community Resource Officers that have the Emergency Equipment (Emergency Lights) above use it on accidents
The service-oriented workforce known as Community Patrol & Investigations (CPI)

Hands Up!

can be used to hold down traffic accidents; obtain descriptions of suspects or person of interest in crimes without getting involved physically. The new Model of Community Policing is allowing Community to Lead without interfering and causing vicarious liabilities to increase.

The training will extensively focus on intervention skills with Cultural Intelligence playing a key role in developing communities.

For some, working as a volunteer can lead to employment. Yet, the initial purpose of this service group is to remain as the Eyes and Ears while maintaining confidentiality of certain actions that will be taken by the authorities and any information divulged will be investigated no matter how minor.
Some Police Agencies are affected financially; and the administration may be task with enforcing Immigration and those escaping immigration through Migration.

Community/Police Relations involve allowing the people residing in the community with access to telephone number; people they can trust; personnel whose integrity can be characterized as an Orange County Sheriff known as Sheriff John Mina.

Hands Up!

His town is running effectively and efficiently. Crime may rear its ugly head; but it is often found, and crime will continue to spiral down because he understands community/police relations.

The Civil Wars in Black Communities throughout the Country can be solved by allowing them to serve as helpers or CPI. Community Relations is essential.

Community/Police Relations

In some agencies, seeing how may traffic tickets can be given in a month time. In some cases, Beer is the bet; whiskey or money. The supervisor allows that type of behavior to permeate the agency because "it is only a motivator," he replied when asked about it.

The fact that the more Auto traffic Citations are written, the higher automobile insurance and home-owner insurances and soon other prices increase. It starts with citations being given NOT because they ran the traffic light; but because they had a cracked windshield that the person who wrote the most tickets won the divisional prize.

Community/Police Relations is far from such antics. It involves gentle conversations, mutual understanding, trust, partnerships; moreover, communication. When communication breakdown, CPR goes.

The way to create a sustainable community that works with the police, it is imperative to begin training personnel from the start of the academy or in-service training a way of executing Community/Police Relations as the approach can be successful but the officer engaging must remain aware of the area.

The reasoning is to win on the streets within the community and neighborhoods by teaching citizens about the difference between Police/Community Relations & Community/Police Relations.

Many professionals and politicians perceive Community/Police as Police/Community Relations. They both have their steps in reducing crime. Community/Police Relations works when the community become the eyes and ears as said of the neighbors and the agency. The community responds with helping the police. They report suspicious activities beforehand.

Police/Community Relations is when the police respond to the community or neighborhood by calls to 911 calls after things happen. Police Agencies are sometimes understaffed as many officers are exhausted. Some agencies who use the terms Community/Police – Police/community interchangeably.

The terms are wrong in their theory when applied interchangeably. Every situation

Hands Up!

community/police is not the approach. But each situation does not warrant police/community relations.

Police/Community Relations practice is what cost the life of Michael Brown, an unarmed black teenager, was shot and killed in the street on Aug. 9, 2014, by Officer Darren Wilson, a white police officer, in Ferguson, Mo. The term Police/Community Relations approach collectively breeds riots.
Thus, the police strategy used to respond to interrupt crimes using police/community relations has received a failing grade. The traditional role involves police barking orders at the citizen or suspect(s) after individuals and community groups refuse to cooperate with the law.

Individuals observe violations but refuse to be truthful in cases. The traditional role Police/Community Relations usually ends with unresolved issues and crimes that become cold cases because of the inability to relate to subcultural groups. Citizens must respect the law, even if the first command feel disrespectful. Just listen! Some citizens believe that they control the police.

An example of police/community relations "if the store owner calls the police and police is late, the store owner tries to reprimand the officer for being later or give to early.

However, the officers involved could have listened to his plea that he could not breathe. Nonetheless, that is NOT criminal. Soft hand combat is allowed when suspect(s) do not comply with legal orders.

Garner could have left the corner rather than challenge the authority. Garner illegal dual labor economy approach to feeding his self and family is NOT a reason to violate the laws such as using an illegal practice to subduing suspects verbally resisting. Community/Police strategies would have been effective with CQ communication.
Most officer(s) on any force initiate aggression as the director of Internal Affairs. The Professional Office of Responsibility did find that the Officer in the Tamir Rice incident was wrong.

The toy gun has been around decades. Nonetheless. Community/Policing Methods were practiced more decades ago than today's times. down after playing with a toy gun in the park in Ohio. The appropriate preliminary investigation and Community Policing could involve the of the P.A. to gain the teens attention. Police Emergency Light is an attention getter. Shooting him was not an option as the agency agreed.

Hands Up!

"Do you want to die by the hands of Mookie?" As the Police Recruiter align his eyes with your eyes to make the point that it is dangerous being a police officer, heart palpitations start. Upon leaving the Gun Range, most cops are ready to put the threat down as taught. But when we use words like (Mookie) is used, anyone can only visualize a Black Boy or Black Man committing a crime like trying to kill you or someone else. Who knew the mind-set of the Officer who killed Tamir Rice in the park in Ohio? There was enough time to investigate and de-escalate the situations with a preliminary investigation while concealing self with cover behind the cruiser before firing the deadly shot in poor judgment.

When did playing in the park become unaccepted? A preliminary investigation could have prevented a senseless shooting and murder that has NOT seem to be prosecutable. The escalation of force should have been enough probable cause to seek an Affidavit of Arrest. Even his past police duties reflect that no CQ training was given. As shootings like Tamir Rice and Michael Brown transpired as well as Eric Garner, many agencies began receiving community pressure and ways to justify actions other than a written-reports or eyewitness accounts. Nevertheless, black Officers have probably gun down more Blacks than White

56
Hands Up!

Officers. But the Media refused to examine the number of times Black officers shot their gun or killed a Black man.

The technology was introduced in 2013-2014, guesstimating that the Body Cameras would be the problem solver. The Body Camera is just as good as the Police Chief who choose to save you or sacrifice you.

The technology thought to be a one idea shut all mouths only produced talks about budgets and 4th Amendment; as well as 1st Amendment questions – constitutionality. Nonetheless, Police Body Cameras are here. The Body Camera are not bad; but now we or police have the ability to record the conversations between Husband & Wife; Boyfriend /Girlfriend as partners are counted as well when they attack the officer or make statements that can be the difference between Innocent and Guilty.

Police Unions and Administrators who sought to keep their men and women out of the public eye when they are innocent were body cameras.

Fortunately, the Body Cameras prove to be effective as some officers were caught planting drugs (Detroit Free Press 2014); other incidents showed Tamar Rice being shot to death in a public park with a toy gun.

Hands Up!

It proved that the Officer had an opportunity to de-escalate the incident and save a child's life. The shooting of Brown prompted protests that roiled the area for weeks.

The "US against THEM!" perception and exhaustion of criminal-economic and social injustices perceived by both sides did not clear up the marching. As BLM marched, the Civil War in nearly every poor or poverty-stricken community of colors, gun fire is taking the lives of innocent children, teens, adults, as the Civil War has been raging on since 1930's.

Where unemployment is the highest in communities and neighborhoods, researchers will discover violent crimes and crimes that distort and disrupt the stability of the community or neighborhoods in poverty. It is imperative that police officers responding to the vicinity under control of criminal spirits seeking to make the wide areas patrolled more violent. Police/Community Relations used as a methodology to reduce crimes is antiquated as the era of young music; the need to feel respected, and the NRA.

Law Enforcement responding with black-gloves and dark glasses with multiple weapons X2 clos by their Departmental Weapons. The military style grade of weapons in the community can only be blamed on the person actually bringing them into the neighborhood.

Hands Up!

Each time a shooting occurs as a Mass Shooting in no-colored communities, the National Rifle Association is blamed. But as the Blood shed riddled with the stench of Civil War between People of Color – the NRA has never been the subject of any Black daily shooting. Therefore, the N.R.A has nothing to do with shootings. People who decided to commit crimes happen to gravitate to a weapon with the mind-set of using a certain weapon without the NRA approval. The NRA does not give Approval to go and kill another man or woman for no reason or his or her own reason is not the NRA job.

The day the I was appointed Chief of Police at around 9:13a.m., when I received a face to face with the Criminal Investigation Bureau (Captain) who informed me that my eldest Son had been killed after 4 people shot him 13-14times. As the Chief of Police, it was my job to apprehend the killers. But by no was I was going to give a press conference and blame the shooting on the National Rifle Association N.R.A. The membership and lobbyist groups may be powerful, but they do not personally advocate violence on inner cities or schools.

People see the police coming as a gang to arrest innocent people or whoever seen to be in the way or in the area as cruisers blaze down the streets looking for shooter instead

59
Hands Up!

of getting the victim to the hospital and the crime scene secured. The incidents and the perceptions paternalistic and maternalistic people being in the area is needed if false.

The Police/Community Relations strategy used currently in majority of America within urban community and neighborhoods is no longer effective due to the trust being broken between minorities and police agencies. Neighborhoods needing to be controlled by 2nd and 3rd shift aggression due to 911 calls and violence plaguing the cities across America.

Endangering communities of color and forcing businesses and schools as well as people with gainful employment out of the urban areas is only going to increase crime. When we examine the urban American cities, we see Leaderless Civil Wars that have no date of ending. Many minorities are unemployed as well as youths. Adults with families and money to survive urban communities usually leave the cities because of Police/Community Relation strategies.

Chapter 8
Work in Progress

The adverse impact is the more traffic fines and tickets that are issued; arrest not solved, breaking and entering because the police are busy harassing the citizens, the more future lay-offs and police corruption is going to transpire. The strategy P/C/R's force innocent people and the alternative result is police lay-offs due to the removal of business stimulating people and schools.

The Chicago Police Agencies are a good example for all of us to learn that criminal activity continues as the Chicago Police use the inept strategy Police/Community Relations. The Police Commissioners over decades have put in practice police strategies that are ineffective and outdated in this era. Police/Community Relations as a strategy to reduce crime is NOT working. It appears that the Chicago is getting worse.

The prosecutors assigned in investigating crimes are the best; but a Police/Community Strategy geared up for urban combat is NOT the way to muster assistance. The way to muster assistance is using the people who are unemployed to act as Eyes and Ears and if essential, provide CBG Funds to relocate faithful volunteers to report adequately on crime in their previous home or living vicinity.

C/P/Rs model was not involved or actively being engaged in the Michel Brown case sought as the perpetrator was viewed as a common thief who deserved to die after stealing candy or chips, soda from a convenient store while citizens and officers are fatigue and some with PTSD that may cause the Officer(s) or Citizen(s) to inappropriate react as decisions are wrong; and riots are flaring upas a result..

The prosecutor of Ferguson, MO announced that a grand jury would be deciding the fate of Officer Darren Wilson on whether to bring an indictment for manslaughter or 1st Degree Murder as evidence of the need NOT to use deadly force was the right thing to do.

Thus, the agency and prosecutor worked out a deal for Officer Darren Wilson to retire or resign with hid pension but without a state charge or federal indictment. The prosecutorial presentation in the evening was political grandstanding when C/P/R's is the answer.

Community/Police Relations can urge the Police Agencies to educate, inform and train agencies and rookies out of recruit school the proper way to approach citizens when 911 is used or if the officer is simply making positive contact with the community whenever there is an incident or no incidents.

Hands Up!

Community/Police Relations is NOT able to be articulated to agencies due to the dinosaur effect.

The dinosaur effect is when the past status quo controlled by police administrators who use controlled employees who will continue with the old dinosaur practices known as Police/Community Relations that aims to alleviate effective communication; and substitute the essential actions for a quick solution such as arrests.

In contrast, the correct methods for this era is Community/Police Relations in the Urban and all communities. Ferguson Prosecutor new ideas of policing; instead CPR Training, politicians urged hiring of a Black Chief of Police to quell the racial component and widen politics as a preservative of maintaining office. The politics or politircks are usually temporary for quick order. Otherwise, citizens and police will become more divisional.

Chapter 9
HUFF & HATE

The announcement set off another wave of protests after the Grand Jury announced that it would NOT be charging Wilson with Homicide.

The decision made by the Grand Jury caused numerous protests to cross jurisdictional lines as it seemed as though that Black men and teens were under attack nationwide. The live target or bounty practice were literally on every black male's head as some subcultural groups began spreading.

Groups like Black Lives matter backed by someone who wanted to cause chaos and confusion paid leaderless groups to champion for a cause unknown. People who wanted to react after the media begin political pandering to achieve ratings. BLM until many of them were identified and found to be criminals. Movements throughout the U.S. seem to be catching fire with agitators. Agitators discovered in the movement was activated to create trouble rather than peace. Yet, the positive news of people feeling heard for the first time was echoed throughout the Black communities who were later dismantled and placed on the HATE GROUP list.

The racial minority communities in Black America and Latin America were allegedly supported – but no agenda existed. The matter of racial equality became the subject matter as BLM allege members ran on stage to impose and intimidate U.S. Presidential candidates 2016 U.S. Presidential Election as the winner U.S. President Donald J. Trump's narrative was to bring the country under the guise of patriotism as **Challengers such as Sports entities, politicians and those uncertain of America could leave America.** The President blunt stance for patriotism surrounding kneeling or placing one's hand over their Heart for America lifted spirits. The patriotism of Military Veterans and those serving died for us to walk freely and do many things other countries are forbidden to exercise. His blunt solution caused the NFL owners to ban the famous Quarterback Colin Kaepernick from ever playing again although many white and black players in the NFL stood along together against Police Brutality, but less penalties were imposed against minority players.

The President wanted to make a statement that we are a nation of laws. The statement spoke to community/police relations event succeeding President Barak Obama who supported the same philosophy but the practice by white officers seem to be the target of hate. As mentioned earlier, Black

Hands Up!

Officer targeted Black Citizens to escape. create chaos as white officers became the problem for some people that are uncontrollable during interaction(s)?

However, it was a real fear of being shot by police and police being shot by citizens became credible. Support of police organizations across America began an outcry for heroes because they are tasked with performing a serious and dangerous jobs. While many people run away from someone firing bullets (rounds) from an automatic weapon; the police run toward the gunman or terrorist seeking to do harm.

This heroic duty to protect people must be acknowledged. In addition, groups like Black Live Matter will NOT march down the street of Chicago where Black gangs kill. for sport. The newly elected US President demanded players of the NFL/NBA owners punish players for disrespecting the US Flag during the National Anthem without articulating why the 1st Amendment was being crushed.

The whole situations took away from issues as that needed to be examined.

BLM is looked at as being non-patriotic was the focus of many debates and subject maters on news outlets that led to penalties by NFL owners who collaborated on fining players who engaged in kneeling during the National Anthem.

In contrast, LeBron James who is one of the most premier basketball icons of our time today in the conversation of Michel Jordan joined the protest vocally. He was later told the "shut up!" and dribble by a conservative neo-con host of Fox News. The players were seeking to gain world-wide attention; and get the United Nations to condemn the killings and human rights violations of Blacks.

The BLM group interrupted candidate's speeches etc. Law enforcement officers in various cities, counties, rural areas and inner-city jurisdictions all use different methods of calming racial violence methodically dispatching their police personnel in fear of loss of life by zealots and members of groups who advocated hate by using hate speech against police. This political grandstanding only pushes us all far apart from a goal that is achievable. Instead, certain groups – even White Supremacist Groups are creating panic and fear as they train with weapons and kill people in crowds.

"Black Lives Matter" who marched for months and chanted various slogans were ineffective due to having no real strategies or conversations for possibility other than race bating the Right or Whites who may be seeking peace under the chaos brewing as the Right Conservatives aggravate matters. Neither group can contribute to the better society that we can be together if we

Hands Up!

understand intercultural communication as well as cross cultural ethnic and cultural relations that help build communities as well as favor with law enforcement agencies.

They (BLM) received exactly what they set out to do as the group is now listed as a Hate Group. Shooting and various racial motivated speech drew the Nights of the KU KLUX KLAN and various Arian nations or followers who condemned (BLM) as well as the media.

Multiple police shootings continued into 2015-2016, 2017, 2018 & 2019 as the now defunct members were found to be criminals themselves looking to retaliate or simply bring attention to themselves. Certain leaderless followers were arrested and incarcerated; followed on Social Media; followed by plain clothes law enforcement. Officers used subterfuge as a subversion tactic to gather intelligence. Members of the group were being questioned due to criminality and their own background by police legally. The subterfuge is essential to root out possible terrorism on America.

One incident involved an undercover officer pulling out his weapon after being made out as an uncover police agent. Rally/Marches as groups from the ultra-right and BLM moved law enforcement to protect life and property. Effective Community/Police Relations – even with an agent working to gather intelligence is proper and necessary. The media showed the officer in a bad light as he used his weapon as the group intended on attacking him.

The undercover officer was shown by the media like he was angry. The paper and television showed him pointing his weapon at individuals or crowds of people. Due to his life being in imminent danger - anger can transpire – yet, it is not helpful when bias media outlets use stories that can get people to buy racism or bigotry lives in police liaison officers patrolling our schools in the U.S., instead of misdemeanors and felonies.

The school resource officer according to CNN footages of a White Police Officer in uniform with a body of a body builder at the request of the teacher, the resource officer slammed her down! Thereafter, he {Officer} picked up the young Black teenager as she set at her desk seemingly texting via cell phone while ignoring his commands on school property. He slung her around the classroom inside of the student's chair as though she was at a carnival.

The school resource officer continued twirling her as the Fox News/CNN footages show the teenager being jolted from the chair and thrown onto the ground. He handcuffed the young teenager and arrested her. His actions by using corporal punishment. The

Hands Up!

force continuum ideology belongs on the street and not in the classroom where our children are told they are safe; and each day is one we all can learn from as people.

Prior to the 18th, 19th, Century, black men and women enslaved were policed by Slave Patrols on Horseback with shotguns and whips to coerce forced labor without wages directly benefiting the family or individual.

Some Police/Sheriffs benefit from placing police officers in schools. But the political grandstanding is the like the Civil War - North and South within America as disrespect for one ethnic group is widely practiced with ideology of supremacy.

The school resource officer must retrain individual students who are violent. Community/Police Relations is the current methodology that should be practiced by every police agency desiring to reduce crime. The young children whose mothers and fathers were using drugs and drinking alcohol beverages are responsible for the new wave of violence. Young teenagers who become adults remain violent because no one ever sought to teach them the difference between felonies and misdemeanors.

Yet, the school resource officers wandered around the schools seeking for employees to protect him. The old behavior such as School

Yard to Prison Yard started after the first arrest of juveniles in the past to shape mentalities such as the Resource Officer. Thus, it is important to develop a great relationship with your Community/Police Officer because mistakes happen NOT crime. The Officer should examine if the crime or nuisance is a need to see rom a School Resource Officer attitude and behavior of a criminal? Do the community want to see our children protected? The Work in Progress or WIP is a way to gather all the finest communicators within your department and articulate how to impact communities without causing them to work against the department personnel.

The WIP looks like Officers walking on foot on certain days and meeting with the block club leaders in the community and going to door to door on down times; and get to know the neighborhood leaders to express their interest in building the community and city by reporting with their eyes and ears.

After defining the leaders, assigned officers distribute their phone numbers of the division to remain in close contact with leaders to commence Proactive policing and reduce 911 emergency calls Patrolling the Streets or COPS Program as it was known years ago should be revitalized & revamped.

Chapter 6

71
Hands Up!

Convict Leasing

Black enslavement and Jim Crow era may have been rebranded and the new enslavement and ways to gain wealth by leasing convicts for employment purposes without payment to convicts, but to the police, courts or corrections.

In the past, the imprisonment of Blacks throughout America, especially in the South as they continue controlling people of color by escorting them down the street while on Horse Back – even this day. Moreover, they learn to make material that can be sold but sent to the manufacturer in exchange for money given to the Police, Judge or Warden.

When U.S. President Nixon was a candidate and then President in the 1970's – Nixon became known as the champion of "law and order." His tactics draw Southern state votes. The tradition of going back much further than the Civil Rights era in Alabama in 1870 Blacks comprised of 74% percent of the prison population, but only two-decades before, they had been just 2 percent, (Lopez, p. 38). Slavery ended in 1865 by the signing of the Emancipation Proclamation in 1865 to solve slavery and commerce without reparations for the slavery.

Slavery is said the begin August 31, 1639 – August 31, 2019 (equals) 400 years of

Hands Up!

slavery. Indentured and unqualified servants fresh out of slavery returned to the plantation to work for some place to stay as a Black family. The term known as carpet baggers triggered throughout the South. Thus, Slaves were free per control but not per their minds. Soon, after the food and shelter was not enough, criminal nature transpires – even today as centuries has past, oppressed minorities often avoid recidivism.

Mass Incarceration levels increased dramatically. According to Lopez, Blacks enslaved by whites were depicted as contented, happy, frivolous, and foolish – in short, childish behavior.

The need for paternalistic guardians in the form of an owner and master may still be alive. Once White Supremacy is identified in film, TV, radio or in commerce, people with paternal views ought to get involve with helping people who are lascivious, dangerous, but primarily afraid of competition can be corrected. Blacks and Latinos are painted as being joyfully enslaved in poverty. It was post-emancipation that brought those views-points. A threatening stereotype quickly became the engine that would steer one (whites) into becoming economically well-off from convict leasing by Law enforcement; Courts & Corrections System. The criminal justice system was used to support wealthy families and increase impoverished employees on the inside to become wealthy as the term **"convict leasing"** was a way of life.

It became the ultimate wicked tool for individuals and governments to increase the Gross National Product (GDP). The benefit in gaining currency; and Whites becoming wealthy are partially why 97% of wealth do not belong to non-white people.

In establishing control, almost every black was in collusion with law enforcement to win the respect or help stop other slaves from escaping. The type of Community/Police Relations often helped commerce maintain its stability. Those who obeyed their masters were often spared of death; but those who revolted such as Nat Turner et.al experienced death.

The families of revolutionary people saw gender & racial hostility increase. Genocide of Blacks by KU KLUX KLAN coerced blacks into involuntary servitude for 400 years. The need for paternalism was established as slavery never ended until August 31, 2019. Many people are unaware of their spiritual freedom and physical freedom if you work with the police, courts and corrections by not engaging in criminality. The Civil War was certainly political; and the cattle worth fighting for were enslaved Blacks in the South. But in general – the United States Constitution, the Black Race is framed as One/Third { 1/3rd } of a (man or woman). The Constitution declare Blacks as unequal to any other race; and the framers never thought that the world would evolve through education, information and training in the area of Constitutional Amendments. The ghost of slavery never ended. Blacks make up the most ethnic group imprisoned

Blacks seemed happy and content per Lopez (38). The Constitutional Amendment framing Black Americans who were enslaved for over 400 years to be amended by standing up to our forefathers and stating that they done a marvelous job in establishing the Bill of Rights; but North American slaves were free to work as humans.

The 21st Century revealed that prominent leaders of our Government has continued ignoring not only that Blacks are NOT cattle; or 1/3rd of a person; but due to the mass projections and eras throughout the centuries, relief have not been granted – beginning with the U.S. Constitutional Amendment of renewing our thoughts and coming to a full understanding of inter-cultural relations. Cultural communication or cross-cultural communication that can establish relations.

Hands Up!

Respect can be garnered if rural school teach that at least 100 of inventors were Black Americans enslaved and free. Yet, establishing respect under paternalism is not working and has not worked for decades.

Everyone contributes to history rather they are doing it within the subculture or in the view of other in society. The beautiful cities, counties, rural and agricultural building of living conditions are maintained because of people value of history.

Blacks and Whites who died for freedom and the causation of equality; and those who continue living and fighting for racial equality and gender equality are trying to close the wealth gap as a result of slavery as well as the commerce that was taken from native people such as the stop traffic light. Racial minorities subject to **"Black Laws."** were hurtful, inhumane & traumatizing too. Black Laws prevented Blacks from obtaining wealth; marrying outside the race; or leaving the plantation. The crime for escaping may be Black babies being cut out of stomachs for their husbands seeking to flee the plantation for freedom. Also, in Florida, many babies, teens and adults were fed to alligators after they were caught wondering in Florida in wicked places that were racially insensitive.

An engine search of Blacks being fed to alligators in Florida at one time or now was a real deal. The respect of human life was not considered. But history will also show that One man known as Benjamin Banneker laid out the foundation for Washington, D.C. as well as the Father Time Clock in London, England.

The Civil War birthed Black folk fighting alongside their non-wage paying employers (sic) Masters until Abraham Lincoln's E.O.

Chapter 10
TEAM PLAYING

A great majority of Black & White Lives were lost; and the wealth of Whites from convict leasing may be present. and present. The laws today in reflection along with relief to stomp out tension and the evil spirit of racism or racial prejudice against racial minorities and poor Whites Americans.

Re-introducing Community/Police Relations curriculum and explaining the purpose without viewing it from post-racial viewpoint can help educate, inform and train LEO's.

Community/Police Relations that is strikingly different from Police/Community Relations as we tried to convey the difference in the introduction is what is wrong with agencies who seek grants that target hard core areas is **Police/Community Relations. The target areas are mostly drug related.**
A plethora of politicians and law enforcement personnel have heard of police/community strategies that offer grants for crime areas; but it is essential to select the right dedicated police personnel to implement Community/Police Relation Program. The strategies will help neighborhoods stand on their own without the use of Guns or Weapons. The approach supposed to develop relations and give communities a chance to stand on their own.

Community/Police Relations and preparing to launch a program or policies surrounding the subject matter must be examined to see if the community understand the difference. It is imperative that everyone knows the difference between the two terms. One focus on arrest; while Community/Police Relations focus on building relationships based on trust and mutual responsibility. Prior to engaging, citizens must have a background check.

When leaders or lay person use the terms interchangeably, there must be some type of double planning to that deploy both strategies. The difference is where the patrol investigations and police interventions, arrests, and police presence as well as adequate response times to situations or incidents can be used interchangeably, but the leaders and followers of the program are to remain in confidentiality.

However, when police personnel arrive on scene and bias attitudes, physical exertion, name calling, unnecessary authoritative commands; grabbing anyone within the crowd and throwing them into the police vehicle along with pepper spray (chemical) use and police batons to punish the suspect(s) or innocent witnesses is why police/community relations is being challenged by citizens and high profile personnel.

Hands Up!

Dispatching the police patty wagon to arrest and collect as many DNA samples as possible within communities is harsh but only if the program is compromised and shootings or crimes skyrocket.

Under the same circumstances such as police investigations, patrolling communities, police interventions, police presence without arrests, name calling, police shootings, chokings, provoked police shooting or provoked arrests and unwilling physical exertion, instead – trained employees with skills to negotiate and de-escalate attitudes and behaviors without the use of force; pepper spraying (chemical) use to control the suspect(s) or innocent people; the patty wagon, Community Leaders and followers should know exactly who to approach being a part of the team Together Everyone Achieve More with Community Police strategies being deployed constantly.

Hands Up!

Chapter 11
Attitudes and Behaviors

Patrolling and Administrating as law enforcement officers can trigger PTSD or Post-Traumatic Stress Disorder even if C/P/R's is being practiced. Thus, exercising and eating the right types of food; and drinking plenty of water as well as seek to educated in Intercultural and Cross-cultural Communication.

In predominantly & ethnically **White** Communities, it is almost positive that the person closest to the culture or subculture, the Officer with that identity usually takes the lead on the call or being flagged down for an incident. **"Community/Police Relations is practiced as the officers that was often observed during his rookie years often chose soft tones; alternatives to arrest and conducting a conversation vs being on edge. If appears the officer(s) are secure.** Many Black Law Enforcement Officers who have partnered with non-black officers and assigned to White communities rarely arrest. The arrest rates are lower even though the same crime(s) or intimate spouse abuse/Domestic Abuse occurs in communities of color.

In matters such as kidnapping hostages, Malicious Destruction of Property within his own culture coerce the White Office to tell

Hands Up!

the Black Officer(s) **"I will handle this call."** Cultural identity plays a significant part in White Communities in which White police are called via 911. The Black colleague often waits in the patrol squad car. One hostage with handguns begin shooting at police with the intent to gain the attention of his wife.

The suspect was yelling and screaming because his wife had filed for divorce – it was his only chance to save his marriage on rocks. The **"Community/Police Relations" tactic** used to gain a favorable outcome and building relationships with people residing the community seen a violent episode end in an empathetic way.

The SWAT Team arrived as the hostage negotiator began speaking through the megaphone seeking to negotiate the suspect out of the home although he shot several rounds at them from within the home in Michigan. The law enforcement officers were very disinterested in killing the suspect. And they did not return fire to initiate a fire fight.

Upon examining the best way to get the hostage to stop becoming aggressive – the brave police officers used community policing methods to gain total control of the situations. It turns out that his wife was a Director of a Social Program and highly connected with politicians.

Chapter12
Communication

Police/community Relations in Urban areas often fall due to the inability to communicate with various subcultures without displaying racial bias or fear of the unknown. Most surprisingly, many recruits are programed to arrest **"Mookie" Blacks.**

Interagency Disputes

Reflecting on historical disputes and bias ideologies within police agencies by superior ranking officers trickle down to middle managers to patrol investigators experience police personnel aggression due to the inability to communicate in subcultures that has been shown to have racial ideologies, or racially inferior. An uneducated police or citizens with no cultural understanding, intercultural communication, or bigotry in their heart and mind muster back after work at "Choir Practice."

Choir practice is when the shift is over and the officers meet in an undisclosed location and use alcohol, drugs, or their choice of illicit items and disclose stories of hate, bigotry, plans to arrest, who or where the money or graft is located.

Even in the squad car a difference in how smooth the day or night shift runs depends on the ability to communicate. For example, in some white officers in their communities are

Hands Up!

kind. In communities of color, their communication skills quickly lost causes the uninformed person of interest to become fearful when they have done nothing. The tone of voice and language used by the officer engaging in cross-cultural communication is harsh and disrespectful in some agencies.

Their superiors are residents of the community of certain personnel assigned to their community where protection is ordered. If the police partners are not on trust terms, communication is stifled and sometimes the uncomfortable officer will request to return to the station to take the day off; or request another partner.

Things like that occur if the colored officer does not do what is requested such as leave the room for a deal that would keep the person committing the crime out of the lockup. The **(colored partner) making decisions that would hurt** non-white families may need a supervisor because the non-white officer feels like an arrest is essential, but his partner do not. This experience and bad encounter with the agency officer cause long term negative relationships. Bias behavior never make sense to superiors. David Livermore, Ang Soon wrote about communication and how effective communication can build relations when honest, open, and integrity is present.

Linn Van Dyne, PHD's - the description of low power distance is that the agency leaders expect that all should have equal rights. Also, in low power distance, the idea of being willing to question and challenge the view of superiors in seeking to rid interagency disputes. When the agency has disputes that are sensitive, the problem or issue is kicked down the road for another day.

Interagency disputes along with racial bias and disharmony over the numerical arrests in the Black vs White communities still exists. The leadership sets the tone of how policing methods are dispatched. Although American police agencies outside of America, organizations practice Low Power Distance in Austria, as does the United Kingdom. But within some police organizations in the U.S., the leadership is High Power Distance philosophy within police organizations; and low and High-Power Distance theory.
High Power Distance expects power holders to be entitled to privileges; and the idea leaders are willing to support and accept the views of superiors. Thus, a inept and culturally uneducated force are more prone to Police Brutality.

Today, if you are reading this chapter to Hands Up "A Guide to Community/Police Relations" – it is passed time for us to work together. The Community and Police can make great contributions to lowering crimes while maintaining their civil rights to own guns and ammunition. Guns are NOT stumbling blocks; it is education, information and training on how to use the weapon for those who qualify to carry firearms.

Every time there is a shooting, whether mass or minor, the liberal politicians and some public lay people along with leaders begin bashing the National Rifle Association. (NRA) has very little do with attitudes and behavior of Gun Violence in the community or anywhere. Law enforcement officers desire is to quell violence. The reduction of crime while police shootings is viewed as criminal in every shooting is a false narrative.

"Community/Police Relations" with unbiased leaders who respect communities. Police Administrators have opportunities to change attitudes and behaviors by examining how leadership set the tone on how policing is conducted. Low High or High Low Power Distance are only theories – but in theory, many Commissioners or Police Chiefs must understand how to use their position to improve the interpersonal relationships; and subcultural communication training with a chance of avoiding problems by helping the citizen consider that the authority if distinguished will destroy the Criminal Justice System due to tension in relations.

Hands Up!

Chapter 13
Cultural Intelligence

American organizations who practice CQ knowledge and abide by Low Power Distance and Source Selection in the hiring category often have reduced citizen complaints due to community/police relations.

There are some people of certain ethnic groups who have never experienced spoken with people of color or Latino Americans. Also, television depiction of Blacks, Hispanics, and non-whites whose only interaction is through TV that they learn false depictions about various subcultures.

Portrayal of violence amongst Black men, teens and children are inundated throughout the news media, movies, daily TV programs and real violence within the subculture as the leaders stand around and discuss violence. Citizens within the communities are faced with backlash of low CQ from the police officer as law enforcement are faced with low CQ from citizens who choose to trouble the officer by challenging the authority in which they are given. Thus, upon encountering people who are depicted as violent, the natural reaction is to save your life if violence transpires. But when your Chief advocate racial animosity, the community if further put on notice that we cannot trust the police.

Hands Up!

For example, on June 5, 2019 in the 21St Century, a Black News outlet (The Root) reported by Monique Judge (writer) for the Root found that some agencies allow their personnel to vent on Face Book citing First Amendment Right "Freedom of Speech" but when speech goes too far then the leadership is held accountable for the behavior. The Root reported that police personnel used Face Book as **"Police Officers Get Exposed For Making Racist Social Media Posts, So Cities Decides to What to Do? Root Investigated:** An up to date article on law enforcement officers who use Face Book.

As their right to voice their bias and racist views as public servants are now at the center of an investigation.

Ms. Judge investigated and sought to bring to light those public servants who work for the taxpayers – but hate the community who pay the taxes: Ms. Judge wrote the following article that introduces the need for unbiased leaders, including Human Resource Administrators (Hiring Managers) to screen out those public servants who use their free time to verbally and vehemently attack the people who pay their salaries.

After the employee who published on Facebook, the public posts of those individuals made who found thousands of Facebook posts.

The comments that ran the gamut from racist memes to conspiracy theories to bombastic expressions of violence.
Several officers expressed the desire to use a taser or deadly force on suspects, actions that have brought law enforcement under scrutiny in recent years and sparked nationwide protests police brutality.
African American singer Sammy Davis Jr. in an apparent dig at the Black Lives Matter movement. The image was shared on Facebook in 2015 by a captain.
According to Judge and others, hiring the right law enforcement officers are the only way to correct issues that challenge the U.S. Constitution via Face Book Posts. Judge said, "We are supposed to believe that law enforcement officers view everyone the same and treat everyone fairly under the letter of the law."
We are supposed to believe that, but we know deep in our souls that it's not true." Police officers and departments across the nation have been accused of having implicit bias against and racist views about black people for a long time. The accusations are not new, but they are often refuted by those accused. No training in

Cultural Awareness or intelligence will lead the citizen or officer into miscommunication.

According to James W. Neuliep, reducing conflict is necessary; and conflict is inevitable...

We can, however, through cooperative intercultural communication, reduce and manage conflict. Often, conflict stems from our inability to see another person's point of view, especially if that person is from a different culture (p. 8).

Urban neighborhoods and communities of color are out gunned by armed forces (National Guards), City police, local Sheriff and Slave Patrol KU KLUX KLAN NIGHT RIDERS in the past as well as today should reflect, review the past harm, restructure police policies and deploy culturally aware police personnel and community. It has become too common today for communities and police to avoid the tough conversation for possibility using strategies. The refined approach will possibly de-escalate police/community violence. By citizen aggression or police escalation and brutality. and if we do not come to some form of resolution as an anti-violence program as well as positive community/police relations strategies that will save lives of our tax paying citizens and law enforcement officers, more violence will transpire.

Hands Up!

In 2019, the leadership or Chief/Police / Police Commissioners being appointed by Mayors or politicians who share the same racist ideologies that are appointed in many cases. As reported previously, if the leaders do NOT value every life – the sentiments will trickle down to police personnel who will gradually adjust to being comfortable with using language and behavior non-conducive to building relationships. For instance, in the State of Florida a Police Chief in Miami directed his staff to engage in explosive and horrific behavior as the Chief of Police as he urged subordinates to falsely arrest those accused while stacking the charges.

Miami Herald News Reported

A former police chief in a Southern Florida suburb has been indicted for pressuring his officers to pin crimes on any African American with "somewhat of a record" to keep the crime stats in his jurisdiction perfect. The Miami Herald reports that Raimundo Artesian created a racist culture in the Biscayne Park Police Department that targeted black people, **(Helm. 07/04/2018)** which shows unconscionable and most likely illegal practices allowed.

The marching orders were discovered after investigators began examining the arrest tally of Black Teens and

Blacks in general. The Miami Herald reported through the author (Helm). Certain officers adhered to the orders. It is possible that some of the teens or men arrested became targets if certain burglary crimes or other violent crimes that were unsolved to be picked as the persons responsible for the crimes they did **NOT** commit.

Miami Herald News Reporter: Helms investigative reporting revealed that the Chief informed his subordinates of the following: "If they have burglaries that are open cases that are not solved yet, if you see anybody black walking through our streets and they have somewhat of a record, arrest so we can pin them for all the burglaries."

Anthony De La Torre said in an internal probe ordered in 2014, "They were basically doing this to have a 100% clearance rate for the city" and such actions cannot be tolerated.

In a report from that probe, four officers — a third of the small force — told an outside investigator they were under marching orders to file the bogus charges to improve the department's crime stats.

Only De La Torre specifically mentioned targeting blacks, but former Biscayne Park village manager Heidi Shafran, who ordered the investigation after receiving a string of letters from disgruntled officers, said the message seemed clear for cops on the street to engage in bias traffic stops and arrests.

In the author's experience, Black Officers were often seeking to charge citizens with crimes to garner overtime to pay for their toys even if they had not done anything. as the words were exchanged while in the cruiser. One Officer sought to find an item like a broke crack pipe to charge the person with being in possession of illicit contraband.

Chapter 14
All Lives Matter

Education, information and training in Cultural Intelligence (CQ) will prevent kidnappings of citizens, killing individuals as we hear and see the inner-city violence as police respond repeatedly to violent crimes.

The leaderless organization known as the Black Lives Matter Movement are marching and creating attention when the urban areas of every city, violence is perpetrated against the person who most look like themselves. Like crabs in a basket, many urban citizens in poverty with no education often get involved in minor then major criminal activity.

NYPD personnel have had numerous leaders who were conservative and liberal. Yet, in urban communities, violence is high. Officer in every agency may deal with drug traffickers, gun dealers (illicit) contraband.
It is time for Black leaders and White Leaders and Latino leaders to stand up against violence everywhere. **All lives matter** as BLM seek to focus on White Police to easily demonize an ethnic group without enough research. Thus, it is imperative to turn up traffic stops (legal) and non-bias stops and continue performing their jobs. People who deceive the masses of people by immediately focusing on the actions of Whites are wrong.

Most cops understand that positional power can influence behavior and actions of police.

All Lives Matter as each officer respond or initiate a deduction in crime by intervening when suspicious activities are present in neighborhoods and communities. Ethnic minorities need to focus on community interventions within their own jurisdictions or neighborhoods to reduce the violence or nuisances such as e.g. spray painting the exterior of businesses or cars on the lawn.
In Chicago and Detroit as well as Memphis, the violence amongst Blacks against Blacks is like unto a Civil War. The Civil War is primarily due to perceptions and lack of education, information, training, and employment within the community or city.

In Philadelphia where multiple Officers were shot and wounded - social media was inappropriate as the violence was allegedly condoned by community members, and others outside of Philadelphia. Speech or behavior that approve violence against police or first responders when others run away.

Thus, it is important that citizens be empathetic to first responders (Police) and (EMS) or (Fire) who are responsible for health & safety of the public remain calm and listen to every order given by the officers as citizens involved reduce possible casualties

95
Hands Up!

instead of criminal activities. Hate speech against law enforcement is wrong as well; and should be an ordinance or law. It is feasible that some law enforcement officers and citizens belong to public services understand that taxpayers deserve great police services or public servants that care.

According to The Root and Miami Herald, it appears that Hate Speech and Hatred displayed by racial violence will continue to spark attention and damage relationships.

Cops or citizens who work alongside domestic terrorist, hate groups initiate investigations and it may become prejudice.
History: In reflection, various politicians – whether Democrats or Republicans as well as other non-recognized political parties knows that the slavery of blacks was wrong; and to continue politicizing the matter without solutions is the status quo.

CQ can help reduce or change a person's attitude and behaviors. The skills can bring clarity to the officers' and citizens hearts and minds. **"Black Lives Matter"** called a Hate Group were successful in proposing that **Officer Darren Wilson of the Ferguson, MO. PD be discharged well after the shooting of Michael Brown.**

The political climate caused him to want to resign, but the acts of violence continue in Saint Louis, MO as some politicians in both parties believe the firing of Officer Wilson was right thing to do to quell the violence and marches and rioting and looting stores to get attention in the U.S. The group **"Black Lives Matter"** marched throughout the streets of North America, but mostly within the inner cities. **"Hands Up!"** and **"Don't Shoot!"** going unrecognized as leaderless followers as the leaderless group is defunct.

Nonetheless, **BLM** marches have no legitimate strategies or reasons to loot stores, homes, and burn down businesses as well as tuning over vehicles after setting them on fire is NOT organization; it's terror. In a few cases, 'Black Lives Matter" cause was found to be fraudulent and without legitimacy. Some of the people who seek attention by going from city to city to be on the local or national news outlets made the small contribution of exposing injustices; but they were committing crimes too – even though many of the participants sought to hide within the group while sparking the riots.

It is widely known that the group who is defunct while leaderless followers are being monitored and arrested for crimes from their past crimes. The felony/misdemeanors charges negate the fact that they do not have

Hands Up!

a legitimate purpose. Some were charged with conspiracy to riot and thefts; while others are still under investigation due to the destruction of property.

The group's lack of leadership skills within the subcultural communities with their own BLM group allege police brutality and police oppression; but evidence of targeting Whites as the suspects as they defend their own lives as they seek to return home to their families.

One issue need addressing is that every 25-years racial minorities such as Black Americans or African Americans et.al must rely on Congress to pass the **Voting Rights Act is more of an issue to march on streets. All Lives Matter, thus, it is imperative that Voting Rights be permanently restored is a matter that BLM can march for rather than demonizing the police and disregarding the violence within their own communities to reduce homicides.**
U.S. President Obama in 2008-2016 had an opportunity to make that happen. But the moment Trayvon Martin was shot in 2014, the U.S. President refused make the Voting Rights permanent. All Lives Matter as we approach 2020 elections.

Now, as our country appears to be re-entering racial tensions as immigrants resist using the proper protocols to enter the United States of

Hands Up!

America. Border Agents (ICE) have a right to restore law and order but Custom Officers are scrutinized and given poor media coverage as the U.S. President provide moral and logistic support on a complex issue that has been lingering in every political administration as immigrants continue to evade border control.

The immigrant crisis can be solved if Democratic or Republican politicians take a stand with the president without trying to entrap the U. S. President with lies.

Chapter 15
Understanding Entrapment
Entrapment Case #1
People v Jamieson, 436 Mich. 61; 461 NW2d 884 (1990)

In People v Jamieson the Michigan Supreme Court asked for briefs to determine whether they should abandon the objective entrapment test in preference to the subjective test on September 12, 1990, they concluded that there was not enough justification or need to change a settled law in Michigan.

They did, however, reverse the Court of Appeals decision who found that Jamieson had been entrapped. Jamieson, a juvenile went to a sergeant in a county jail and said "jail guards were bringing controlled substances (narcotics) to the inmates inside the jail facility. The entrapment case became a precedent for other cases that would come after the high-profile entrapment defense. After meeting with local authorities, the sergeant was given 10 days to devise a plan to apprehend the correction officers involved. A reverse sting or take back sale operation was chosen.

The juvenile was to approach a correction officer and request that he bring narcotics into the jail facility. However, the juvenile was not instructed as to approach and as a result of these operations – five deputies (defendants) were arrested and charged with delivery of cocaine.

The trial court found entrapment and the issue was appealed to the Court of Appeals who upheld the trial court's conclusion that defendants were entrapped because the juvenile had the "unfettered power" to select grist for the judicial sense as Court Ruled. Nonetheless, the Supreme Court reversed holding that five deputies were not entrapped. The decision was because the conduct of the police was not a governmental manufacturing or inducement of criminal conduct but served only to provide the defendants with the opportunity to plan new crimes and oppose law & order. Law enforcement traps are very common. The internet (NET) is a tool that easily captures those involved in crime(s) and those potential threats.

Two Types of Determinations May be Used: Subject vs. Objective

The **subjective** test is authorized by the United States Supreme Court and Federal Court System. It determines entrapment is based on the entrapped person(s) (defendant(s) willingness, character, state of

101
Hands Up!

mind, conduct, and past illegal acts. The **objective** test is used by Michigan and other states within that circuit. The objective approach is an inquiry based upon facts. Unlike the subjective test, the objective test does not focus on past convictions.

The objective test can be said to lead to a fairer assessment. In addition, the objective approach enables judges to analyze and correct the past actions of the police; thereby helping to defer future police misconduct. When the involvement in criminal activities goes beyond the simple offering, and when police conduct may induce or instigate the commission of a crime by a person not ready or willing to commit, regardless of the character of that person – entrapment may have occurred.

How is entrapment determined

❖ How did the defendant respond to the inducement?

❖ What were the circumstances surrounding the illegal conduct?

❖ What was the state of mind of the defendant before the entrapment offer?

❖ Was the defendant already engaged in similar or existing illegal conduct before the entrapment?

❖ Did the defendant premeditate the crime before the government's involvement?

❖ What was the defendant's reputation?

❖ Did the Office seduce the target?

❖ Was the target complicit without receiving information about the crime?

❖ Were any of the defendants trying to change their minds prior to engaging in criminal activity?

JUDICIAL

COURTS

Chapter 13

Judicial Courts

History will prove that both Democrats and Republicans owned Black slaves and was in complicit in having White servants work off their debts. Prior to the evolution of racial ethnic & relations, a significant foundation of America's Judicial System (Judicial Courts), the Great Biblical Leader known as Moshea or (Moses) Hebrew was Anointed and Appointed by the Almighty Eternal GOD as Priest, Prophet and Judge of the People of Israel.

The ideology built by the Judicial System can be found in Exodus 18, 19, 20 (NIV, 2017). Moses met with the Priest & Father in Law of Midian who offered Moses advice for more than 600,000 people in the Wilderness outside of Egypt. The 600,000 or more people had no rules and regulations or laws that govern the conduct of the behavior.

The antiquated laws in that era transpired after the chosen leaders were having difficulty judging their tribesman or tribeswoman innocent or guilty by two or three witnesses. The large tribes often caused dissension and the leader would take the allege violator before Moses who would be coerced to solve the civil or criminal problems between parties within or outside the tribes of Israel.

Moses Father in Law advised him to become a participative leader amongst over 600,000 people. From Lawsuits to Criminal Wrongdoing and how to live with Integrity amongst one another was taught to each leader to teach the people of his Tribe, including his and her children are to be taught the Law and Rules/Regulations and ordinances in order to physically live. Once they followed the law, they were without blame and there was no need to see the Judge.

Once the LAWS were administered to each person, they were responsible to follow the law by pursuing justice. Justice was the ONLY way the people were to pursue because the pursuit of justice is the Commands of God (Elohim.). If a matter could not be established by 2 or 3 witnesses but probable cause existed, the alleged party would be taken to (3) Judges (panel) equal to the District Courts in some Circuits. Thereafter, the Judicial System became more sophisticated and many foundational principles were removed from the Court Rooms or premises altogether.

Decades ago, the US Supreme Court, equal to **(Moses)** deriving at findings Divinely observed Yahweh Elohim (GOD) write the (10) **Commandments. which** are not welcomed inside of any of the United States Courts due separation of church & state, but is foundational laws established laws/Courts.

The Laws and Statutes that make up America really came from GOD. Our Judges have Judicial Authority to punish the guilty as Moses and the 12-Tribes of Israel did in their day. Moreover, the punitive measures were much more severe in nature and Spirit to continue after adopting significant precedents or cases decided to be against nature or spirit is Murder.

Murder in past times required one be spared but left to wander outside the City without any benefits of an upstanding citizen. We call them fugitives from justice. In some States today, the Death Penalty still exist because of the Laws of God & Moses. Judges were established and cases that Judges reviewed and overseen in those days can be read in the Holy Bible in Exodus and Judges et.al. When we decide cases, our Judges should be aware of the historical precedents biblically setup.

In some cases involving law enforcement officers and accidental shootings; or unjustified shootings, now is the time for our U.S. Judicial System become highly aware of Post-Traumatic Stress Disorder (PTSD), (PTSD) which may be one of the diagnosis of certain police personnel and/or citizens whose actions were triggered due to one or repeated exposure to trauma and stress.

"Dog Whistle Politics" and the need for money or funding should be the least of our worries. Mental Health is on the rise and it does not know occupations or colors or people. **Mental Health in the form of PTSD is one of the reasons why the book Hands Up America was written.**

Our Judicial System must become very familiar with various mental health and work with legislatures to rule on police & citizens.

When it comes to Judges ruling in the Courts on subject matters relating to mental Health because it is a growing issue that is costing billions of dollars in efficiently operating the Courts; at least in the future it will become.

If the Courts does NOT specifically address how to efficiently and effectively deal with offenders who are Mentally Ill, a severe precedent will transpire for Judges to finally address the issue of Courts and mental health. The issue is significant because the sentencing guidelines and where the person should or should not be confined after committing crime(s) above local ordinances is a matter of the State of Mind *(Mens Rea)*.

Those in authority will exceed their Judicial Powers if practicality is not laid down to offer help to the mentally ill who may commit crime like mass shootings of schools. The sentencing guidelines help Judges stay fair.

Hands Up!

The sentencing guidelines must be re-written by the U.S. Congress; and some portions of it have already been revised by the Oval Office as his Executive Orders took effect. Many Federal Offenders were released for minor crimes or major crimes involving drugs due to being substance abusers as well as drug sellers.

According to Martin Kelly, "the first actions of the newly created Congress were to pass the Judiciary Act of 1789 that made provisions for the Supreme Court." The Courts often decided cases that did not divide people. But in around 1789 the Judiciary Act:

> It said that it would consist of a Chief Justice and five Associate Justices and they would meet in the nation's capital. The first Chief Justice appointed by <u>George Washington</u> was John Jay serving from September 26, 1789, to June 29, 1795.

Hands Up!

The five Associate Justices were John Rutledge, William Cushing, James Wilson, John Blair, and James Iredell. "Code Term" or systematic early warning system to keep a tight control on decisions and other or dockets defined human rights in Dred Scott Court Case.

Dred Scott was an enslaved African American man in the United States. unsuccessfully sued for his freedom and that of his wife and their two daughters in the Dred Scott v. Sandford case of 1857, popularly known as the "Dred Scott case". Scott claimed that he and his wife should be granted their freedom because they had lived in Illinois and the Wisconsin Territory for four years, where slavery was illegal and their laws said that slaveholders gave up their rights to slaves if they stayed for an extended period. This case is out of Sanford, Florida.

The Supreme Court used its power and understanding with empathy and sympathy but used their common sense to rule on the right side of history as the justices ruled to allow Dred Scott and his family go free because the laws or the future laws based on the Dred Scott Case changed the way people examine various enslaved Blacks to the United States Courts website, there is a difference between the Court System.

There is Federal and State Courts as well as District Courts. The U.S. Constitution is the supreme law of the land in the United States. It creates a federal system of government in which power is shared between the federal government and the state governments. Due to federalism, both the federal government and each of the state governments have their own court systems based on the Constitution of the United States of America.

Hands Up!

If we seek to discover the differences in structure and judicial systems according to Peter Blair, The U.S. court system is split up into two distinct sections: state and federal courts. These two types of courts vary in several important ways, how types of cases handled. The accepted cases and the sentences they are authorized to give in key differences between state-level and federal courts: The courts have a much broader jurisdiction case.

Federal courts, on the other hand, only have jurisdiction in certain situations, such as when: The United States is a party in the case if the case involves a violation of the U.S. Constitution. The case involves a violation of federal laws the case involves citizens of different states and the amount in questions exceeds $75,000 then the Federal Government of a certain Circuit or jurisdiction will assume control of the Case.

Hands Up!

- If the case involves bankruptcy, copyright, patent, or maritime law out whether the case should be tried in state or federal courts.
  - As a general rule of thumb, the federal court system will have jurisdiction when the case involves (1) more than one state, (2) some sort of federal system - (U.S. Postal Service). (3) It occurs on federal property, such as a national park or military base, or (4) involves a violation of the U.S. Constitution or other federal law. In certain cases, both state and federal courts can choose whether to pursue state or federal court Caseload

  - Since state courts handle such a wide variety of cases, they typically have a much heavier caseload. There are approximately 30 million cases filed every year in state court.

115
Hands Up!

In the Federal Courts the number may be more than compared to the state courts by possibly more than 1 million in federal court cases. Therefore, state-level cases may take several months or even years to run their course, while federal cases tend to follow a more streamlined path. And while federal courts hear fewer cases than state courts, the cases that have significance with Penalties or jurisdictional matters.

- When tried in federal court, crimes carry much harsher sentences after someone was arrested for <u>trafficking. Heroin in California</u>. Under Health and Safety Code 11352, the accused would face a maximum of five years in county jail, fines, and probation.

- On the other hand, sentencing guidelines need reforming in the Courts for those arrested for example trafficking the drug heroin in the U.S.

116
Hands Up!

The (Schedule I drug) trafficked across several states and state lines and say crossed into California, if tried in federal court, the accused would face a minimum of 5 years and a maximum of 40 years in prison for assuming the amount was not more than 1 kilogram, it was only the person's first offense, and it did not lead to serious injury or death, which come with sentencing enhancements.

Establishment of State and Federal Courts: State and local courts are established by a state (within states there are also local courts established and other municipalities. Federal courts are established under the U.S. Constitution to decide disputes involving the Constitution and laws passed by Congress.

Jurisdiction of State and Federal Courts: The differences between federal and states. The courts are defined mainly by jurisdiction.

Jurisdiction refers to the kinds of cases a court is authorized to hear. State courts have broad jurisdiction, so the cases individual citizens are most likely to be involved in -- such as robberies, traffic violations, broken contracts, and family disputes -- are usually tried in state courts.

Federal court jurisdiction, by contrast, is limited to the types of cases listed in the Constitution and specifically provided for by Congress. For the most part, federal courts only hear: Cases in which the United States is a party; cases involving violations of the U.S. The Constitution & Federal laws under federal jurisdiction in question.

- Federal laws (under federal-question jurisdiction);
- Cases between citizens of different states if the amount in controversy exceeds $75,000 (under diversity)
- Bankruptcy, copyright, patent, and maritime law cases will be assumed.

118
Hands Up!

In some cases, both federal and state courts have jurisdiction. This allows parties to choose whether to go to state court or to federal court. **Criminal Cases in State and Federal Court.**

Most criminal cases involve violations of state law and are tried in state court, but criminal cases involving federal laws can be tried only in federal court. We all know, for example, that robbery is a crime, but what law says it is a crime?

By and large, state laws, not federal laws, make robbery a crime. There are only a few federal laws about robbery, such as the law that makes it a federal crime to rob a bank under federal law. Examples of other federal crimes are bringing illegal drugs into the country or across state lines and use of the U.S. mails to swindle consumers or acquire drugs against federal and state law.

A neighborhood association brings a case in state court against a defendant who sacrifices goats in his backyard. When the court issues an order (called an injunction) forbidding the defendant from further sacrifices, the defendant in court as an unconstitutional infringement of his/her freedoms.

Some kinds of conduct are illegal under both federal and state laws. For example, federal laws prohibit employment discrimination, and the states have added their own laws which forbid employment discrimination. People can go to federal or state court to bring a case under the federal law or both the federal and state laws. A state-law-only case can be brought only in state court.

Courts and Caseloads: State courts handle by far the larger number of cases with more contact with the public than federal courts do as they hear far fewer cases than the state.

Hands Up!

Think of the court cases you have heard the most about. Most are U.S. Supreme Court decisions, because the federal laws they uphold and the federal rights they protect extend to everyone in this country.

A case usually begins when a plaintiff files a pleading with a trial court. For the sake of simplicity, this article focuses civil cases, however, most of these concepts also apply to criminal cases. A pleading, although different in form from jurisdiction to jurisdiction, will contain claims or charges. The plaintiff brought a Civil Case against the Defendants. Richard accused David of stalking him when Richard had not seen David in nearly 0ne-year.

In Richard pleadings, he claims that David made him fear for his life and job security. Thus, he requested and injunction order for one-year although David hadn't seen him.

Hands Up!

The Circuit Judge ignored all evidence that vindicate David under Fla. Sta. 741.030 that admonished plaintiffs in Florida that in order to obtain a Restraining Order, the plaintiff must have been threatened or violence occurred within 6-months of filing the I.O.

Richard never proved the Burden of Proof brought by the Plaintiff who must present evidence consistent with his story. The false claims or charges filed on the Affidavits is criminal and is referred to as Fraud on the Courts. The crime is rarely punishable in the State of Florida. Restraining Orders that disrupt the Judicial Process with the scheme on the Court Documents (Affidavits) in the of Law the Court Clerk should be have a duty to initiate prosecution. The Federal or Circuit Assist. Court Clerks handle all the paperwork filed. Richard (brother) lied in the Courts without reason or rhyme and was dishonest.

Hands Up!

The case ended but Richard lost his State Employment and sought to continue retaliating against his own flesh and blood. David sought a restraining order but by then the Court had drawn the conclusion that the Case should be inside of the Civil Courts of Claims.

Many people who do not have financial freedom and suffer from Poverty or lack of financial resources can be placed in the Court System after violating a traffic signal if the system desires you off the street. I small cases such as Civil Litigation involving restraining orders; if a Judge initiate your guilt, it will take an attorney at law or someone over the Judge to reverse the Court Error immediately.

In large cities like Sanford, Florida where the young teenager Trayvon Martin was shot, cases involving Restraining Orders are being used to develop a Criminal Record.

Chapter 14

Court Sentencing

Sentencing

The post-conviction stage of the criminal justice process, in which the defendant is brought before the court for the imposition of a penalty. If a defendant is convicted in a criminal prosecution, the event that follows the verdict is called sentencing.

A sentence is the penalty ordered by the court. Generally, the primary goals of sentencing are punishment, deterrence, incapacitation, and rehabilitation. In some states, juries may be entitled to pronounce sentence, but in most states, and in federal court, sentencing is performed by a judge.

For serious crimes, sentencing is usually pronounced at a sentencing hearing, where the prosecutor and the defendant present their arguments regarding the penalty phase.

Paul Reynolds: First off, thank you for having me. When you can have more bodies in prison, obviously, you're going to make more money off of them, cutting costs. Violations and other minor charges, sentencing is either predetermined or pronounced immediately after conviction. Sentencing in the United States has undergone several dramatic transformations. In the eighteenth century, the sentencing of criminal defendants was left to juries.

If a defendant was convicted, the jury decided the facts that would affect sentencing, and a predetermined sentence was imposed based on those findings. In the late eighteenth century, legislatures began to prescribe imprisonment as punishment, replacing such punishments as public whipping and confinement in stocks as the C.O.'s who impose punishments until the owner(s) force continuum policy to be discontinued.

Hands Up!

Beginning in the late nineteenth century, legislatures began to pass statutes that left sentencing to the discretion of judges who may be a part of the convict leasing program. This movement toward indeterminate sentencing allowed judges to order a sentence tailored. Under sentencing statutes, a sentence could be any combination of **Probation**, fines, restitution (repayment to victims), imprisonment, and community service. Judges were allowed to consider a wide range of evidence in fashioning a sentence, including **Mitigating Circumstances**.

In the 1950s, Congress passed a spate of federal legislation requiring that judges impose mandatory minimum sentences for drug offenses. These laws directed that defendants must serve a minimum number of years in prison upon conviction for certain offenses – Judges did not have control.

In the 1960s, these laws came under attack for failing to deter drug crimes; moreover, prosecutors refuse to prosecute. Criminal Justice Reform emerged, and many argued for longer prison sentences, and they also pushed for uniformity in sentencing, noting that discretionary sentencing produced widely various sentences for the same crime to maintain status quo.

Several states' legislatures enacted sentencing guidelines in the 1970s and early 1980s. These guidelines increased punishment for criminal offenses and limited judicial discretion in sentencing by identifying the punishment required upon conviction for an offense.

Under many of the new sentencing statutes, **Parole** for prison inmates was either abolished or restricted to certain offenses as conservatives achieve victory over liberals.

Following the lead of these state legislatures, Congress passed the Sentencing Reform Act of 1984 (SRA) (Pub. L. No. 98-473, 98 Stat. 1987 [1984] [codified in 18 U.S.C.A. §§ U.S. In the case 3551–3556 (1988 & Supp. V 1993)]) as prisoners' get off granted for good behavior, the precedent was established. The SRA also established the **U.S. Sentencing Commission** (USSC) and directed it to create a new sentencing system (28 U.S.C.A. §§ 991(b), 994(a)(1)-(2) [1988]). Between 1984 and 1987, the USSC crafted the Federal Sentencing Guidelines. Since Congress did not object to the guidelines, they became effective on November 1, 1987 (28 U.S.C.A. § 994 [1988 & Supp. V 1993]).

The Federal Sentencing Guidelines shift the focus from the offender to the offense as guidelines categorize offenses and identify of the sentence required upon conviction allow Judges to increase or decrease sentences.

The reasons on the record for departures, or increases in sentences, are easy to achieve under section 1B1.2 of the sentencing guidelines. This section allows the sentencing judge to consider all "relevant conduct," including the circumstances surrounding the conviction, offenses that were committed at the same time as the charged offense but were not charged, prior convictions, and acts for which the defendant was previously tried but acquitted.

In limited circumstances, judges may decrease a sentence. For example, a judge may downwardly depart if the defendant accepts responsibility for crimes committed. Prosecutors often challenge the decrease sentences on appeal, and they usually win because the guidelines call for adherence in all but exceptional cases. Prosecutors receive tremendous discretion in the sentencing to impact the minds of others and politics.

Hands Up!

Under the guidelines, prosecutors can easily increase or decrease a sentence by tinkering with the number of counts either in the initial charge or pursuant to a plea agreement. For example, a prosecutor may not use evidence of certain conduct in pursuing a criminal charge.

However, upon conviction or a guilty plea, the prosecutor can, in the sentencing hearing, introduce that evidence to increase the defendant's sentence at this point, if the prosecutor, Judicial official work together. EVIDENCE presented in the case can show the defendant committed the acts and the court is obliged to increase the defendant's sentence due to being a habitual offender.

Furthermore, state police officers and prosecutors can make secret decisions about what cases to refer to federal prosecutors. State prosecutors can thus pressure defendants to enter a guilty plea in state court.

The decision on whether to move the court for a downward departure in exchange for substantial assistance to law enforcement is also left to the prosecutor desk and agenda.

At first, many federal judges refused to recognize the Federal Sentencing Guidelines. In *Mistretta v. United States*, 488 U.S. 361, 109 S. Ct. 647, 102 L. Ed. 2d 714 (1989), the U.S. Supreme Court held criminal sentences. As part of the Comprehensive CRIME CONTROL ACT of 1984 (Pub. L. No. 98-473. Title II, October 12, 1984, 98 Stat. 1976 to 2193), Congress passed legislation requiring mandatory minimum sentences for drug and firearm offenses (Pub. L. No. 98-473. Federal Guidelines 503(a), 1005(a), 98 Stat. 2069, 2138 [1984] [amending 21 U.S.C.A. § 860 (formerly § 845a), 18 U.S.C.A. § 924(c)]) exist. As we consider scaling back progress, many inmates are still innocent of the crime(s) they are accused of doing.

In 1986, as public fears of drug abuse increased, Congress enacted the Anti-Drug Abuse Act of 1986 (Pub. L. No. 99-570, 100 Stat. 3207 [1986]) to create mandatory minimum sentences for drug trafficking. minimum terms. In 1988, Congress broadened the mandatory minimums to cover conspiracy in certain drug offenses (Anti-Drug Abuse Act of 1988 [Pub. L. No. 100-690, § 6470(a), 102 Stat. 4377 (21 U.S.C.A. §§ 846, 963 [1988])]).

The 1988 act also established a minimum sentence for simple possession of crack cocaine and the suspect's luck of being unarmed or without contraband. Under 21 U.S.C.A. § 844(a) (1988 & Supp. II 1990 & Supp. III 1991), a first-time offender caught with five grams of a mixture. A "cocaine base" must be sentenced to no less than five years in prison. In contrast, a person caught with five hundred grams of powder cocaine

Hands Up!

to receive a five-year sentence (21 U.S.C.A. §§ 841(b)(1)(B) (ii)-(iii) [1982 & Supp. V 1987]). SENTENCING GUIDELINES: FAIR OR UNFAIR Sentencing guideline systems for determined criminal sentences that was dramatically changed in this era. Twenty-two states and the federal government use sentencing guidelines to require a judge to calculate a sentence using a mathematical formula. Points are assigned based on the defendant's offenses, prior criminal record, and other factors.

A total is calculated, and the sentence is computed. A judge has very little room to depart from the sentence mandated by the guidelines. Critics believe that the distinction without differences matters as bias sentencing often go ignored. There has been controversy over fairness and the legitimacy. The sentencing guidelines, with the most criticism directed at the U.S. Sentencing

Guidelines. The criticism comes mostly from defense attorneys and judges, who argue that the guidelines give prosecutors too much power in the criminal justice system and give too little discretion to judges to shape a sentence to fit the individual defendant. Defenders of sentencing guidelines contend inequality. **Arbitrary** and disparate sentencing practices that come with unbridled judicial discretion. Congress authorized the U.S. Sentencing Guidelines in 1984 to continue with unfair sentencing of convicts.

The U.S. Sentencing Guidelines Commission consisting of a seven-member panel appointed by the president and confirmed by the Senate, issued the first set of guidelines in 1987. The guidelines have been constantly changed, mostly by the commission's power. By 1996 the federal guidelines had grown to an 850-page manual with complex formulas.

Proponents of federal sentencing guidelines believe that they reduce sentencing disparity and guarantee harsher punishment for federal felons, many of whom are convicted for selling illegal narcotics.

Before the guidelines were created, the proponents argue, defendants tried to avoid judges who handed out tough sentences and to find one who would be lenient. Thus, in one court a bank robber would get an eighteen-year sentence, while in another a robber convicted of the same crime would receive only five years in prison for unknown reasons; bias & opinion of the crime and who. In addition, there was evidence to suggest that minorities received the harshest treatment under sentencing guidelines have, therefore, reduced the arbitrary dispensation of punishment as supporters lift the project. Many contend that because the guidelines provide predictable sentences, they serve as a

Hands Up!

deterrent to crime. Criminals know the formula of past conviction plus new conviction equals a certain criminal sentence. Criminals no longer can play the angles in the criminal justice system to their advantage but must face a definite punishment.

Defenders of the guidelines also believe that the reduction of judicial discretion reduces the stress suffered by federal trial judges. No longer do judges have to wrestle with their emotions in devising an appropriate sentence. The guidelines provide an efficient means of delivering a criminal sentence public policy. Critics of the federal guidelines contend that uniform criminal sentences may seem attractive, major criticism is the shift from the judge federal prosecutor to the sentencing.

A guidelines, a prosecutor's charging decision is the most important one in the case. A prosecutor can determine a defendant's time in prison is short or long.

Critics argue that prosecutorial discretion has replaced judicial discretion, allowing defendants who hire defense counsel knowledgeable in the workings of the guidelines to negotiate plea agreements that reduce the charges.

Defendants with less EFFECTIVE COUNSEL receive longer sentences. Critics point to the disparate sentences in the same crime. Prosecutors can be bias when applying charges against certain defendants. Critics, like federal judges, decry loss of discretion to shape criminal sentencing federal/state. Mathematical formulas, reducing a human being to the number of points on a sentencing grid worksheet.

Judges forced to ignore certain individual guidelines for prosecutors. Those judges who depart from the guidelines and give more lenient or more severe sentences invariably invite appellate review of their decisions.

Hands Up!

The courts continue to impose severe penalties that are out of proportion to the nature of some of the offenses. In addition, Congress has vetoed some sentencing commission revisions to the guidelines that it has regarded as politically unacceptable. Critics also object to the growing complexity of the guidelines, analogizing provisions. **Internal Revenue Code** as the sentencing commission's continuous revisions and uniformity during the sentencing phase of all convicts – especially if they are habitual.

Three Strikes Laws: In 1994, Congress moved to limit the applicability of mandatory minimums to low-level, nonviolent drug offenders. Under 18 U.S.C.A. § 3553(f), a judge may use the guidelines instead of the statutory minimum sentence if (1) the defendant does not have a criminal history of more than one point (one minor conviction, such as a petit misdemeanor); (2) the defendant did not use violence or credible threats or a firearm in the offense; and did not coerce another to do so; (3) the offense did not result in death/harm.

(4) The defendant was not an organizer of others in the offense and was not engaged in a continuing criminal enterprise (such as a Racketeering scheme or the functioning of a street gang). (5) By the time of the sentencing hearing, the defendant has informed the prosecutor of all the facts of the case. **Also in 1994, Congress exercised its power over sentencing by passing the Violent Crime Control and Law Enforcement Act of 1994 (Pub. L. No. 103-322, September 13, 1994, 108 Stat. 1796). Under provisions of this act, violent offenders convicted of their third felony must be sentenced to life imprisonment (Pub. L. No. 103-322, §§ 70001–70002, 108 Stat. 1796, 1982–1985 [1984] [codified as amended at 18 U.S.C.A.**

§§ 3559, 3582(c)(1)(A) (1988)]). The mandatory minimum Guidelines.

Mandatory minimum sentences remove all discretion from the sentencing judge, whereas the guidelines allow for some leeway. In *United States v. Madkour*, 930. (F.2d 234 (2d Cir. 1991), M. P. Madkour. recent graduate of the University of Vermont with no criminal record, received a mandatory minimum five years in federal prison for the manufacture marijuana. Under the guidelines, the prison sentence would have been 15 to 21 months. The most common punishments the statutes of states impose are community service and probation. Also, fines and restitution, and imprisonment in the 1990s, - presented some southeastern states authorized sentences of hard labor on chain **Gangs**. Many states are trying to reinstate and have the death penalty as the private prisons surfaced far prior to 2020.

The death penalty sentences are now being discussed in various hearings as the judge may consider all relevant evidence prior to imposing the death penalty in today's criminal cases involving homicides.

The RULES OF EVIDENCE do not apply in presentencing hearings, so **Hearsay** and other fallible evidence may be introduced. In both federal and state courts, the sentencing hearing is preceded by a presentence investigation and reports can have a significant value in sentencing. These are conducted by a court services or probation officer, who then submits the report to all parties to the prosecution.

At the hearing, the prosecutor and defendant are entitled to argue against the recommendations for sentencing made in the presentence report. The presentence report can urge a larger sentence for convicts as they may argue with their attorneys representing.

In many states, courts still possess the authority to craft sentences within the bounds of sentencing statutes. In these states, criminal statutes contain a sentencing provision that are minimum and maximum punishments for specific crimes.

For instance, hunting alligators without a license "shall be punished by a fine of not less than $500.00 and, in the discretion of the sentencing court of no more than 12 months. (Ga. Code Ann. § 27-3-19). This means that the judge *must* order a fine of at least $500 and *may* also order imprisonment of up to 12 months.

Many states have also passed so-called three-strikes-and-you're-out laws. Under these laws, when a person receives a third criminal conviction, the person's sentence is enhanced and considerably in. California's version used

142
Hands Up!

the term three-strikes law to make money. U.S. Supreme Court under California's law, if a person with two prior felony convictions is convicted for a third time, he or she will receive a greatly enhanced sentence. Cal. Pen. Code Ann. § 667 (West 1999). Some defendants have received convictions of 25 to 50 years for petty thefts. In one California case, Leandro Andrade was convicted of stealing five video tapes from a K-Mart store. The petty theft charges were tried as felonies, he received two consecutive 25 years. Another case, Gary Ewing, who was on parole from a nine-year prison term, was convicted of stealing three golf clubs. He received a sentence of 25 years.

Both Andrade and Ewing appealed their sentences, alleging that California's law constituted **Cruel and Unusual Punishment** in violation of the **Eighth Amendment** to the U.S. Constitution. The Supreme Court disagreed with both Andrade and Ewing. In

Ewing v. California, 538 U.S. 11, 123 S. Ct. 1179, 155 L. Ed. 2d 108 (2003), the Court held that Ewing's sentence was not grossly disproportionate and, thus, not in violation of the Eighth Amendment.

The crime he committed constituted a felony decision. California legislature to enhance the sentence of a repeat offender was within the discretion of the legislature. The Court also upheld the conviction of Andrade in *Lockyer v. Andrade*, 538 U.S. 63, 123 S. Ct. 1166, L. Ed. 2d (2003). The Andrade's case, the court found that the Ninth Circuit Court of Appeals had erred in granting **Habeas Corpus** relief after a California state Court. The federal law when it ruled that the California statute continued practicing law as the 9th Circuit assumed jurisdiction 3 strikes; opponents of DETERMINATE SENTENCING claim that it will result in increased crowding of prisons and greater costs of incarnation.

Proponents note that the enhanced sentencing will result in long-term cost savings because repeat offenders will no longer be on the streets; but critics point to convict leasing.

These supporters say that the state and federal governments will save on property loss, losses from pain and suffering, lost wages, police security, and medical insurance costs resulting from the crimes of these offenders and there is no research regarding. Some judges who have become dissatisfied with high rates of **Recidivism** have exercised their sentencing discretion and have used other measures such as drug courts and veterans' court to reduce recidivism.

U.S.

CORECTION

SYSYEM

Chapter 15

Prison Pipeline

Innovative punishments intended to address the specific criminal conviction or the conviction history of the specific criminals. For example, a judge in Wilmington, North Carolina, gave a shoplifter the option of serving a prison term or standing outside J.C. Penney with a sign.

In Seattle, a youthful car thief was sentenced to 90 days in detention, a monetary fine, and 16 months of supervision, during which time he was required to wear a sign saying, "I'm a car thief" in the public. The carrying around the sign as people from the community laughed and he became the talk of the community. As he wore the sign over his front shirt in front of a store and was ordered to raise the sign that I stole food and the sign is meant to create embarrassment to avoid sentencing the man to prison.

Critics, including the **American Civil Liberties Union** (ACLU) deplore such punishments as forms of public humiliation. Juvenile court judges possess tremendous discretion in sentencing. In 1995, Judge

Wayne Creech, of the Berkeley County Family Court, in South Carolina, ordered 15-year-old Tonya Kline to be physically tied, 24 hours a day, to her mother, Deborah Harter was an order imposed on Kline and Harter after Kline was charged with truancy, shoplifting, and housebreaking while under tethering conditions could only to go to the bathroom and to shower.

Many Courts from the Federal, State, Local Level within the Judicial System elected or appoint competent judges that seek to regulate the court rooms; respect the defendants; and seek to understand the plaintiff's claim or indictment.

Oftentimes, politicians will appoint individuals that helped them win political contests and contribute masses of money to their campaign. The strategist or philanthropist can even request that individuals be appointed to the Bench after acquiring their license to act as a Judicial Official.

In 2016-2017, and 2018, a Civil Rights Official who works with the Department of Families and Children (DCF) of Florida. His entire actions are unethical and illegally.
The Civil Right Employee sought to make some money because he is incompetent when it comes to managing money. Thus, he created several companies that ultimately depend on RFP's or an agreement to act as a representative in fighting against the State of Florida for $10 million dollars. The employee targeted people who are having a difficult time in coping with life due to illness term.

Hands Up!

Therefore, he created Murphy Services LLC (Settlement Company) that sought to extort money from the Orange County Public School District and Evans High School after it was alleged that a teenager was raped and molested multiple times on the school grounds and off the property. The fraud of seeking to extort OCPSD and Evans High by seeking to privately bring a lawsuit against the District and personnel without the knowledge of the Governor or his own employer.

Once his fraud involving the author's wife was exposed, the author informed him that criminal complaints were going to filed against him. At that time – he waited a couple days until the criminal complaints were filed. On March 13, 2018, he was advised of his possible misconduct by his superiors and fled on March 16, 2018 to the 18th Circuit Courts in Seminole County Florida.

The jurisdiction is Sanford, Florida is the same jurisdiction in which Trayvon Martin was shot dead. However, the courts heard the plaintiff's accusations that he was in fear of his life by the author although he had not physically interacted with the author for 8 months.

On April 9, 2018, the Judge appointed by then Governor Jeb Bush in Florida was assigned to the case. As she considered the hearing for an Injunction Order under 741.30, it was discovered that 741.30 was troubling. After the Judge entertained the case, she heard the evidence from the author's wife in which the facts of the case laid out; nonetheless, the Credible evidence presented from the stand after testimony was rejected. The Judge did not only reject the testimony, but she dismissed all evidence and found that the fact that the author's twin brother had not interacted with him, under 741.30.

For more than 2-years, the incompetent judge continued using her bias opinion and abuse of authority as a Judicial Official that ignored all evidence that should have been considered as she disrespected both defendants in the case. The Judicial Qualification Commission was notified as several canons were violated.

The author used his understanding of the criminal justice system to write various people in authority to advise them of the disrespect; lack of understanding of the Civil Laws in Florida; and the over sentencing of the author's wife with (5) years of an injunction order against her under 784.048 after the missed court date was due to her disabilities; including having Open Heart Surgery at 19 years old. The case was NOT adequately examined as many missteps in Civil Laws in the 18th Circuit Court.

Chapter 16

Grand Jury System

A **grand jury** is a jury – a group of citizens – empowered by law to conduct legal proceedings and investigate potential criminal conduct, and determine whether criminal charges should be brought. A grand jury may subpoena physical evidence or a person to testify. A grand jury is separate from the courts, which do not preside over its functioning.[1]

The United States and Liberia are the only countries that retain grand juries,[2][3] though other common law jurisdictions formerly employed them, and most others now employ a different procedure that does not involve a jury: a preliminary hearing. Grand juries perform both accusatory and investigatory functions include obtaining and reviewing documents and other evidence, hearing the evidence as Grand Juries deliver or refuse.

Hands Up!

Testimonies of witnesses who appear before the body is sworn to silence; and the accusatory function determines whether there is probable cause to believe that one or more persons committed a particular offense within the venue or jurisdiction of the federal circuit. Once the information is consumed, the body can return with a Sealed Indictment (Accusation); or return without delivering an Indictment.

A grand jury in the United States is usually composed of 16 to 23 citizens, though in Virginia it has fewer members for regular or special grand juries.

In Ireland, they also functioned as local government authorities. In Japan, the Law of July 12, 1948, created the *Kensatsu v Shinsakai* (Prosecutorial Review Commission or PRC system), inspired by the American system.[4]

However, the grand jury is so named because traditionally it has more jurors than a trial jury, sometimes called a petit jury (from the French word *petit* meaning "small". Grand Jury pools are continuous and convene often.

The Grand Jury can also be traced to the time of the Norman conquest of England in 1066. There is evidence that the courts of that time summoned a body of sworn neighbors to present crimes that had come to their knowledge. Since the members of that accusing jury were selected from small jurisdictions, it was natural that they could present accusations based on their personal knowledge.

Historians agree that the Assize [court session or assembly] of Clarendon in 1166 provided groundwork for our present Grand Jury system during the reign of Henry II (1154-1189), to regain the crown by force.

Thomas Becket, Chancellor of England, 12 "good and lawful men" in each village were assembled to reveal the names of those suspected of crimes. The pool can hear Civil or Criminal cases and decide to pass on the Bill or Indict.

The oath taken by these jurors if they would carry out their duties faithful that they would aggrieve no one through enmity nor deference to anyone through love, and that they would conceal those things that they had heard.

By the year 1290, these accusing juries were given the authority to inquire into the maintenance of bridges and highways, defects of jails, and whether the Sheriff had kept in jail anyone who should have been brought before the justices. "Le Grand Inquest" evolved during the reign of Edward III (1368), in front of an "accusatory jury"...

It increased in number from 12 to 23, with a majority vote necessary to indict anyone accused of crime. In America, the Massachusetts Bay Colony impaneled the first Grand Jury in 1635 to consider cases of murder, robbery and wife beating as early as the early colonial 1700, values oppose then.

These colonial Grand Juries expressed their independence by refusing to indict leaders of the Stamp Act (1765) and refusing to bring libel charges against the editors of the Boston Gazette (1765). A union with other colonies to oppose British taxes was supported by the Philadelphia Grand Jury in 1770 and the US continues to follow much of the historical platforms laid out outside of the U.S.

By the end of the Colonial Period, the Grand Jury had become an indispensable adjunct of Government: "they proposed new laws, protested against abuses used by government.

History records that public support for Grand Juries, sustained through the Revolutionary Period and began to wane in the early 1800's. Adoption of the Fourteenth Amendment in 1868 was illegal as a Grand Jury can deprive any person of life, liberty or prosperity without due process of law," as interpreted by some states.

Thus, government has the power to wield as a parent wield over his or her children. The tremendous authority in their power to determine who should and who should not face trial " can be very politically motivating. An amendment should be made or reform to the Grand Jury System should no longer be able to bring accusatory charges without a Defense as required by Constitution.

It would seem as though, prosecution of crimes by Grand Jury indictment allow the target fairness due to zealous prosecutors.

Hands Up!

California is still one of the states that allows prosecution to be initiated by either a Criminal Grand Jury indictment or judicial preliminary hearing. San Mateo does not impanel a Criminal Grand Jury on if the Civil Grand Jury ascertains the indictable offense then a separate Criminal Grand Jury will be impaneled.

The first California Penal Codes contained statutes providing for a Grand Jury, to be impaneled quarterly, at the same time as the trial jurors were drawn in early Grand Juries. The role of the Grand Jury in California is unique. The statutes passed in 1880 allowed their duties to include investigation of county government by a Grand Jury beyond alleged misconduct of public officials. Only California and Nevada mandate that Grand Juries be impaneled annually to function specifically in a watchdog capacity over county government.

The striking thing about a Grand Jury that imposes on people's freedoms as the odds of winning a Federal Trial is slim to none. The Federal Government has more money and resources to take a U.S. Citizen or Group.

By the Federal prosecutor presenting his or her evidence called the Government's case(s); and the target often having no knowledge that they are the target of prosecution due to its sworn to secrecy.

If a person or group is called to participate in a running Grand Jury, and they leave the Jurors Box and share who, what, when, where, why and how about the cases that they (Grand Juror) was privy to hear, they will or can receive prison time for **"Leaking information about the Grand Jury."** In some cases, a person can be tried and sentenced to up to 2 or 5 years incarcerated and pay up to $250,000 per Indictment count.

Chapter 17

Penalty Phase

In the United States, it is important that all people regardless of socio-economic background receive fair and impartial sentencing if they are convicted of crimes.

One a person of groups/gangs are convicted in the court of law, especially if the trial was fair, as one person said, "It is all a money game!" He was referring to the Criminal Justice System in every level. The federal, State and local levels of the police, courts and corrections are businesses that used to be public taxes that supported the measures. Also, the revenue from C.O.'s working in the area built the small or large town up as small businesses saw increase in revenue when prisons were being erected. Millionaires and Billionaires received information that Republicans were building private prisons to allegedly reduce the Country's deficit.

Hands Up!

The Gross Domestic Product went from non-human capital to human capital as the farm cattle (Humans) who commit crimes became the target of private prisons. There may be some public prisons within the U.S., but investors were looking for ways to double or triple their money by investing in private prisons to reduce the U.S. Deficit.

The U.S. became the country that incarcerate more of its people than any other country. The reason many believe is that investors like you and others use your capital to invest in buildings that are not controlled properly.

There is noting wrong with investors or those who desire to stretch their portfolio can invest in private prisons or buy a land to build several private prisons. The idea is NOT new, it is a superior ideology that hurt racial minorities who are oppressed and without education and gainful employment already.

In an early chapter, we discussed the issue on convict leasing. In that chapter we discovered that President Richard Nixon was significant in playing a major role in ordinary people with ordinary jobs and families become very wealthy.

We discussed the sheriff or police, Judge, Prosecutors and Corrections Warden or Private Prison owners making a lucrative lifestyle by building private prisons while owning farms to host the new prison. This obvious scheme in the name of reducing the Country's deficit by getting rid of Public Prisons in which taxpayers took a burden with created wealth and wealth gap.

The genocide of certain people by locking them up in prisons in no different than what is happening in the political paly out of immigrants being separated from their families, while others are being lost in jail.

The following critical interview with a private prison correctional officer who was fired for airing this interview in what he called under the "Whistleblowers Act" due to the private prison officials hiring C.O's for much more money was brutalizing and mistreating prisoners, similar to how the "Immigrants" seeking Asylum the wrong way is being treated:

SS: *But if a bigger prison population means bigger profits why would anyone want to rehabilitate anybody at all?*

PR: They wouldn't, and that's exactly what happened when took over a prison. A lot of rehabilitation programs went out of the window; it became a warehouse for inmates, kind of a modern-day slaver if you will.

SS: *Can you elaborate on that? I mean, I'd like to hear a little bit more about it?*

Hands Up!

PR: I guess, why they would want to have more inmates in prisons – to increase their bottom line. It basically becomes an assembly-line form of justice. You get them into system, get them in prisons, and you're warehousing them, you keep them there and you charge the state for incarceration crimes. Basically, there's no rehabilitation when it comes to privatization like this. *SS:* But if things are as bad as you say, why does the government put trust in private prison operators? What's in it for the officials?

PR: I'm sure that they're getting money back. The state is doing anything they can to save money – I don't think they did the time to take the research to do this, so for the States to do this... they're trying to put money in their coffers as well.

SS: Now, the prison you were working in, Lake Erie, it was purchased by the CCA.

Correction Corporation of America CCA
company that owns private prisons was
purchased for 73 million dollars. How much
revenue does it make, that it's willing to pay
that much for a prison?

The term of convict leasing can be very
lucrative over time as the money for
incarceration pays the bills. **PR:** I don't have
that number off the top of my head, I'm sure
we can look that up and find it, but they were
making a lot of money from what they told
us… Once again, I just don't have the answer
for the numbers…

SS: *But do you have, like, an approximate
ration or something?* **PR:** I would say that
with the way they cut programs, I would
easily have to say their revenue or the amount
that was spent on those inmates dropped by…
as an estimate here, I would say, by 30% or
more.

Hands Up!

SS: *Because it does sound like it's a profit for the local taxpayers, if somebody's willing to pay that much money for a prison. Is it a benefit for the people, do you think?*

PR: First off, I think the reason they spent that kind of money on a prison is because they wanted to make this a flagship prison. Private Prisons and a lot of people will agree with the Hands Up that they are overpaid so that they can have the first one in the country, you know, if you're the first one in the country to control prisoners under private corrections, every inmate is going to have their eyes on you to make money as well by laundering money, food, commerce, e.g. cell phones and drugs to survive in the private prisons.

The C.O.'s of Private Prisoners can get caught up in making illegal money just as the owner of the private prisons and certain

Courts seek to make money from sending those convicted of crimes to prison in exchange for campaign or private funding source for their family livelihood.

I think other states have backed away from contracts with them because crimes complicit with inmates were exposed by the media.
The idea that Correction Officers' idea that they were going to make things the best they could and spend all this money and grandiose paydays on obviously, what became an epic failure according to the former C.O.

SS: *Now, CCA says it provides "safe, secure housing and quality rehabilitation programming – and significant savings to taxpayers". Well, the profits of a prison company come from taxpayer's money being paid to them for running prisons. So, are municipalities and states really saving money?*

Hands Up!

PR: No. I would say that they were basically taking advantage of that situation. They're going to come in and take as much from the taxpayer as they can, and when you say that they provide "safe housing" – I can attest that that's not the case. You saw the documentary,

SS: *We're going to talk a bit about that in just a little while, but I want to bring to your attention a report by In the Public that revealed something shocking: it says that Arizona and Colorado, for instance, strike deals with private prisons and the state is obliged to keep its prisons filled up to 100% or taxpayers have to pay the private prisons for any empty beds. So, people must pay for dropping crime rates? I mean, how's that even possible?*

PR: That's... you're not dropping crime rates by doing that. You're going to take somebody who smokes marijuana – let's be honest, and that's not a very crime-worthy. A lot of people do it, police officers do it, who arrest these people and put them in jail – but when the state can say "Hey, you're going to make $2 and you're give us a dollar back for every inmate we give you"… That's sounds like they don't care. once again.

SS: *So, are you saying that people are getting nabbed for wrong reasons to fill up the quotas? Is that correct?*

PR: Absolutely.

SS: *Did you witness that personally?*

PR: I saw some of the inmates they brought in, within the first two months… I don't remember exactly when, within first 2 or 4 months, we had an increase of, like, 500 inmates. Some of these were inmates who were high-level troublemaking inmates, if you will, they had a higher security level.

Hands Up!

Juveniles were completely unprepared. The CCA didn't care, they just want all the bodies to be overcrowded.

One of the reasons is for the money. The longer they stay, the more money the private prison owner makes as the business thrives.

According to the interview, "They, basically, took any of the inmates that other prisons did not want.

SS: *Also, there was a big scandal a while back, the "kids for cash" affair, when a private prison company bribed a county. The owner of the prison would ask the judge to stuff their juvenile prisons with youths. Does having a private prison in an area corrode the judicial process?*

PR: I believe the "cash for kids" was in Pennsylvania, not too far from our prison.

Hands Up!

I am at, and you saw what happened: I believe that judge received 20 years in prison. If I'm in a position of power to make money off something, whether it's gold or silver or people – yeah, I would say it corrodes. I mean, if I can put thousand people in your prison, and you're going to pay me a million dollars – I don't care who I put away, I'm the judge! Yeah, it absolutely would corrode replied one judge caught scamming the system.

SS: *I want to talk a bit more about your personal experience in that private prison. For those who haven't seen the documentary, working at the facility said that you lost your life – why did that happen?*

PR: CCA came in and had a hands-off policy on inmates. The state of Ohio allowed us to use force when necessary to deal with inmates. A 3-to-1 ratio of inmates to CO's.

The CCA said "No, you don't ever touch an inmate, you don't ever deal with an inmate in that way, you don't even use harsh language with an inmate". It only took inmates a few months to realize that we couldn't do our job as C.O.'s.

The CCS took away the C.O.s ability to control, dominate, inspire respect, and invoke a working rehabilitation system. This costed us respect and power in our desire to reform

SS: *Why not?*

PR: Because they were afraid of getting sued. CCA was afraid that if we hurt an inmate, they might get sued and lose money out of their profit.

SS: *They were afraid that they would be sued by inmates who were juveniles and some institutions were.* **PR:** That's correct, yes.

SS: *Okay, but the prison had added hundreds of prisoners after having been privatized. Were there vacant spots to fill? How did that happen?*

PR: Like I've said, they would bring these inmates in, by a busload, to meet their contract requirements to keep that prison at 97%, I believe – I don't remember specific percentage. They just brought them in, whoever would send them an inmate – they would take him, regardless of what this inmate's crime was or his security level.

SS: *You know, I've read that inmates in private prisons beg for solitary confinement for security reasons – how bad is the violence in these facilities? I mean, can you be detailed in your description?*

PR: I was saying, these inmates realized that we could not control them if we needed to, inmates were in control and we lacked power.

Hands Up!

We had a huge increase of inmates trying to go on "segregation" as we call it - to stay safe, and the inmates took control completely. They knew we weren't going to do what we needed to do, and the power balance went from here to here, and it was all in their favor. There was a huge increase of drug activity, violent crimes...

SS: *But why were you scared for your life?*
PR: Because, I was afraid that if I defended myself, I might get thrown in jail.
SS: *Okay, so go ahead, finish about the inmates being scared for their lives...*

PR: ...I was also afraid to lose my job. I have a family to support, I have a child to take care of. But these inmates, were getting their heads bashed in, I used to take them to a hospital. Inmates were constantly fighting as they were robbing each other, extorting each other, it was the Wild West if you will.

SS: *Now, you've mentioned private prisoners being afraid of lawsuits – why aren't state prisons afraid of lawsuits?*

PR: I think that's one of the problems with the States, when they run prisons, they overspend, and there's always been a deficit when it comes to state running anything. That's government for you. I think the lawsuits are easier settled, but remember, we're dealing with government. Some of the costs that coerce private prison owners for are insurance and has liability and things of that nature, so… why was their policy specifically like that?

I don't know, but I think it's a fear of them losing their profits. They've got to make money for the shareholders. If they're not making their shareholders happy, they're not getting new business, not getting into other states, and make this type of money.

SS: *What I wonder is why aren't the state prisons just as afraid of lawsuits from inmates, as are private prisons, like you've said?*

PR: My theory on that is probably because they have a direct pipeline to the justice system. Inmates, who act up in those prisons are likely to face legal ramifications. The unlimited supply of money and, you know, I guess, it also goes back to the balance of power thing I said. These inmates in state prisons are less likely to act up, because they know they might get hurt, corrections officer might have to do things to them that might be unpleasant in order to gain compliance. So, once again, there's much more balance of power in the state-run facility that there is in a private facility. When you tell us that we cannot put our hands on an inmate to gain compliance, if necessary, you give them all the power.

SS: *Tell me something: do private prisons pay less to guards than state prisons? Is there a problem of staff turnover at a private prison?*

PR: To address the turnover issue, there's turnover in any industry, prisons don't escape that in a private run facility in need of money. Correctional Officers can speak for a prison I worked at and some of ones that I know in local area, I can't answer that on a nation-wide level, that could be a state thing, that could be, you know, where are those prisons located, is there enough money to pay these people, but generally speaking, yeah, they're going to pay less, because that affects their bottom line.

SS: *Another thing that struck me is how you said that you were punished for trying to do your job – how so?*

PR: I had to use force on an inmate. I had several of those and they all were found to be justified. I have a degree in Criminal Justice and I did a lot of study on use of force, now there's a use of force continuum that any police officer, any corrections officer, anybody involved with that has to follow, and they're pretty specific by the state is strict.

SS: *What else was wrong with the private prison you were in? You've said before there was lack of medication and inmates sleeping on floors... If a public prison could provide all that, why couldn't the private prison?*

PR: I could go on for hours when you're asking me what was wrong with it, but I'll try to minimize this here. Let's address the medication issue: when CCA came in, the private company who ran the prison, but did not own it, had a system been set up in place for everything to be computerized?

Hands Up!

When CCA came in, they thought: "We're not going to do all this, and we have all this technology, and we're bringing all this, all this money – and they didn't have a computer! When inmates are going to pick up their medicine, the company was like "we don't know where's the inmate medicine at", they'll yell at the doctors and nurses. Everything we learned in training would go out the window. Leadership came totally unprepared to do some of the most basic things I've stated in the documentary, you have some inmates who need some psychotic medication, and if they don't get it, things get ugly.

SS: *What about just other living conditions – I mean, you know, there was also the thing about inmates sleeping on the floor. What, were the beds taken out of the rooms, or the cells, once the prison became private, or what?*

PR: First off, this prison didn't have cells per se; they were dormitory-style areas, housing areas…

SS: *So, were beds taken out of the dormitories?*

PR: No, beds were added to spaces that were normally used for common area, like a common area, quiet room, if you will. They converted those, put beds there. Very-very cramped. There was only about this much space between beds before they moved in, and they narrowed it down to probably like this, you got it right on top of people. So, they added beds. The answer about the sleeping on the floor – that was in segregation. Those cells were meant to hold 2 people at time, and they were housing 3 at a time. You got two beds, three people – somebody's got to sleep, and inmates dictate who does that.

Hands Up!

SS: *What else was the most troubling thing that you witnessed there, except for lack of medication and inmates sleeping on the floor because there were not enough beds for everybody?*

PR: The most troubling thing I saw was the fact of seeing other corrections officers scared to do their jobs, to stand there when incident happens, a fight happens, and officer kind of stand there and go on like this, like "what do I do?" That's scary, because those are people you must rely on backing up if something happens. If I'm getting my rear-end kicked in by an inmate, I hope somebody would step up, but people were asking questions: "Can I do that, or what's going to happen to me and my job?".

It's kind of became "Hey, we've got to watch ourselves first for our own job".

SS: *So, how does a company spend all that money on purchasing prison and then can't provide basic service? Is it incompetence or simply cost-cutting?*

PR: I would say it was incompetence as the money laundering management investigated. "We're going to do it our way. This is how we're going do it, and we don't care what you have to say". They came in with this attitude that they knew it all, but they had no idea. Have they run prisons? Absolutely, okay. But each prison is different. We know those inmates, we know how that prison runs, and they come in and say: "We're going to do it our way or if you don't like it – too bad" – you saw the result of that.

SS: *Now did the inmate behavior change after the conditions worsened like you described?*

Hands Up!

PR: Like I said, it became a free-for-all. The inmates, they just took over and they extorted other inmates and it was out, in the open, the fighting increased. I had plenty of inmates come to me, that I had good rapport with... you know, this is very awkward type of job to be in, you must have certain personality. Would you come to me and say they were scared for their lives? I've run into inmates since I've been no longer employed there and they've said: "Oh my God, it's got so bad!". I departed from there shortly after, within 6 months, and things there got bad after that first year. It got worse after I left, so I can only imagine what some of those inmates were thinking and saying, but the ones that came to me were very scared and very worried about themselves.

SS: *Is there anything you could do for them when they were coming and praying for help?*

PR: Not really. I can tell them to request to go to a different dorm, you could go to segregation – we call it "checking in" – they could do that, but no, there's not much I can do for them. They're grown men, they must live their lives and they have to kind of do things as grown men w/o guidance counselor. Sergeants or just the upper management – let them (prisoner) try to handle it.

SS: *Paul, you know, the picture you're painting is gloomy. So, why is management of private prison neglecting order and control over inmates? Especially, like you say, they are afraid of lawsuits from inmates.*

PR: There's a reason why 6 out of the top-7 managers that were there are no longer there. I go back to "incompetence". They came in there with this "mightier-than-thou" attitude and it failed miserably. I think once the state had to come back in and basically tell them:

Hands Up!

"you're going to do it the way we had it set up to do to begin with" – that prison has run for 12 years without real, major, serious incident or major, serious problems. Every prison has a problem, they all are going to have issues, but to the magnitude of what? First 18 months of them coming in not knowing what's going on, not taking the advice of the people who've been there and, of course, they're trying to implement their system, because that's how they're going to make money for their shareholders.

SS: *According to a study by Chris Petrella, a doctoral candidate at the University of California, Berkeley, people of color are more likely to serve time in private prisons than in public ones. Do private prisons' lobbies target black and Hispanic populations? Did you see more inmates of color?*

Hands Up!

PR: You know, that's one of those statistics I've seen different ways, they talk about African Americans disproportionally placed in prison – I don't know the statistics off-hand, to be honest with you, I haven't researched them in probably two years...

SS: *No, when you were the prison officer, you saw the inmates that were there under your control – were there more Hispanic and African Americans than white prisoners?*

PR: I would say there's pretty good homogenous mix. There might have been a slight percentage, if we're talking, maybe 55% African American, and another 45% would make up Hispanic, white.

SS: *You know, also juveniles are predominantly placed in private prisons, and according to the latest survey or investigation published in Huffington Post.*

They face sexual abuse, also neglect, insanitary food – how does that encourage youngsters to come out and be clean and lead a good life?

PR: Most of the inmates who come in there, juvenile there's really no rehabilitation there. It's a training ground for them. We have shock programs here, in the States, where you send juveniles to boot camps and show them what prison life is really like, but ultimately, I hate to say this, it comes back on the communities to try and change this behavior. These inmates, these juveniles who come in prison, 95% of them come out worse off than when they went it.

SS: *Paul, thank you very much for this interview, for this very sad insight on private prisons in America. We were talking to Paul Reynolds, former correction officer at a private prison, activist against for-profit jails, discussing prison privatization. .S. and*

Hands Up!

That's it for this edition of Sophie & Co, I will see you next time as they would say on the way out of the prison as if they are going to return soon to the private prison as soon as they can find a crime.

New laws surrounding Mental Health and Juveniles will make it more difficult to imprison youth or mentally Ill Adults.

Law enforcement or Officers/Deputies remaining quiet regarding their frame of minds is due to the swift punishment that liberal media outlets bombard the news with as it relates to Police, Court or Corrections.

Therefore, now that we know that there are some bad apples in every category, we must develop an early warning system prior to hiring or appointing or electing someone to a position of authority. The source selection process of being hired should be stringent. A

Hands Up!

A prohibition of denying the life, liberty and pursuit of happiness as well as prosperity in the areas that we need our best must be protected. The Constitution does not hamper the right personnel from being hired, promoted; appointed or elected, it is us who refuse to dig deep into our values to select the right people for positions.

In addition, citizens must be approached, and leaders found as well as followers who are seeking to help the people in their neighborhood with getting the help, we need in Mental Health Therapy.

Confidentiality is important, but ensuring that law enforcement, courts and corrections are aware of diagnoses so that the citizen(s) who commit crimes can be rehabilitated by first understanding their mental health. MH Awareness should always be in our minds when communicating with people.

The opportunity for law enforcement and correction officers getting the treatment they deserve is important too. Critical scene involving injuries or death in law enforcement is NOW!

Mental Health helpers who knows how PTSD effects people in different ways dependent on the traumatic event(s). In some case, the loss of emotional control; use of drugs and/or alcohol, flash backs from the threat of life; nightmares; hypervigilance, paranoia, depression, and many more signs and symptoms that cover Physical, Behavioral, Cognitive and Emotional signs and symptoms of PTSD.

Moreover, intense education, information and training in the area of cultural intelligence (CQ) is not a one shoe fits all, but we know that it is a variable that can work.

REFLECTIONS

Chapter 18

Reflection of the Past

The information and training on Cultural
Intelligence may help police personnel as
well as Citizens if they are committed to
working with law enforcement and other
citizens within their jurisdiction.

Police seeking to help Citizens who request
assistance with nuisance, violent crimes, and
delinquency problems. Aggression is an issue
with the children in the urban areas as they
present problems for their neighborhoods and
communities in which they do not belong.
Many children in Urban vicinities in the later
90's was born addicted to illicit drugs.

The unknown animosity, violent songs
against the Criminal Justice System and rival
gangs make law enforcement become angry
as they are unknowingly handcuff the public
servants who respond by spotting crime. Call

Hands Up!

911 emergency for people & law enforcement in danger. Many citizens do not know what to do, what to say, what not to do or not to say as law enforcement investigate crimes by initiating the crime prevention squad become fearful and many youth or adults run from the police after a traffic stop.

Traffic stops are a significant part of their duties. According to experience and police assistance, drugs, illicit handguns or rifles or other dangerous contraband are seized during traffic stops. In some cases, citizens wanted for violent crimes are apprehended after violating a traffic signal or some sort of traffic violation.

Occupant(s) of the vehicle run, drive away, attempt to run over the police official, or shoot weapons from the vehicle to avoid being apprehended. Regardless of socio-

Hands Up!

economic status or NOT- fleeing is a crime, disrespecting Courts, and Correction Agents. Therefore, this book titled **HANDS UP!** "**A Guide to Community Police Relations**" advocate following the law – including during traffic stops. The first 2-60 seconds within the stop is the most dangerous for the Officer/Deputy first, especially if the stop returned as a felony stop.

The traffic stop is dangerous for the citizens too as he or she may seek to exit the vehicle after the emergency lights are activated. The today's citizen is accustomed to existing the vehicle with a Cell Phone pointed at the Officer/Deputy – which can be mistaken as a weapon. The belief that a driver can exit the car to begin filming the traffic stop to vocalize and show out on their Face Book Account or Instagram Account for others to congratulate them for bravery.

It is NOT bravery to exit the vehicle for fame and weeks of support on social media as **Community Police Relations" is NOT effective or a Work in Progress (WIP) with unfamiliar territory; but it is achievable and is being practiced in various states and cities.** Bouts with crime in communities where people who look a similar (African Americans) who kill one another probably in every city on an daily basis should seek to develop a strong relationship with the department to acquire a community police officer.**

Reflections of violence that pushed or pushes us further away from maintaining health and safety as the goal of keeping people aware that having your **Hands Up is not a sense of weakness. It is simply an opportunity to get to know who patrol your city; but helps citizens learn that traffic stops are teachable moments for citizens & cops.** Effective communicate with officers but listen more than talk. Remember, whatever you say can and will be held against you – especially if you are a wanted fugitive.

It is time that politicians of the U.S. show the world as leaders of the free world that men and women who serve cities, rural and small communities in uniform or plainclothes are upstanding citizens too as public servants.

Citizens who pay the salaries of the Rank and File; salaries for our politicians have a right to be safe in their communities. Law Enforcement deserve to feel safe; thus, implementing Community/Police Relations that involve allowing the citizen to develop ideas and collaborate with law enforcement on strategies. It is imperative that the CPO goes to the Neighborhood Block Club Meetings and be updated on crime in the area to exude collaboration and awareness.

The strategy helps the citizen to depend on one another rather than 911. We do not advocate acting as law enforcement and using your clearance to carry a concealed weapon as reasons to challenge the criminal.

Hands Up!

The police initiating or responding to 911 emergency calls requires citizens to be the eyes and ears of the police agencies or law enforcement departments. Police are public servants, social workers, counselors. Referees outside of the Court etc. The pressure of maintaining order is significant. who serve in dangerous situations, and deserve respect? Whoever told you F...k the Police was wrong then; and is wrong NOW.

Agencies have employees who are learning how to communicate. In every job, there are people who rub people the wrong way as they discharge their duties to care for our public. to learn strategies to develop better relations. For example, some agencies believe that writing more tickets to citizens for head lights burned out; tinted windows, window shield crack, taillight busted, and mediocre traffic citation points only causes citizens to become angry at the police. Earlier chapters informed the readers that taxes increase on insurance, homes, cars, property etc.

Hands Up!

as a result of writing tickets and making complaints of breaking and entering.

Thus, it is imperative to work with the agency. As homes and Cars are stolen due to neighbors refusing to get involved with community disputes only hurts the community. Each burglary, carjacking, shooting, stabbing, assault, rape, or any crimes consistent in a jurisdiction, it is only wise to raise the insurance premiums. The adjustments of insurance premiums that goes up only makes those who can afford to leave the city more reasons to leave the city.

Model City

By the early 1950's, in one of the most renowned cities in America were moving in the direction that most cities desire to do today. Flint, Michigan – which is the birthplace of General Motors brought jobs and stability to the Baby Boomers.

The segregated town of mostly white families had moved from the South to the North; or born in

Flint was able to support their families and relatives with the salary General Motors was paying employees high wages. During this migration, many people who already resided in Flint knew someone who worked for GM and was able to get a job without a high school education.

The city would later be named the model city because the jobs in manufacturing of automobiles flourished, and the Police Foot Patrol Program in Flint was first of many. Schools in the city had various activities for students as well as their families as families were cared for with the assistance of one of the greatest Philanthropist known as Charles Stewart Mott. His organization created a Foundation. known as the Ruth Mott Foundation along with other entities that helped the Model City remain alive.

As time dwindled. People began taking advantage of the manufacturing plants in Flint. Lots of people were taking days off that turned into years. Others were hurt or injured on the job and retired with benefits. During this era, Foot

Hands Up!

Patrol (Police) assigned to communities and neighborhoods became well developed and crime was low.

In the 60's, it was the Mott Foundation that studied research that claimed law enforcement officers that look like the community reduce crime in that areas.

Case #1:

Law Enforcement Officers investigating a late model (four door) with passenger in the vehicles in a community, if an illegal turn or traffic rule is broke, a traffic stop based reasonable suspicion gives officers the right to stop the vehicle.

Probable cause exit due to the care being placed on the B.O.L. The officers' arrest all occupants and its driver.

What should I do when profiling is evident?
- ✓ Turn on dash camera or microphone within your car
- ✓ Put your hands up or on the steering wheel 10-2 as officers' approach
- ✓ Still Cooperate with police
- ✓ Ask officers if you are a suspect of a crime
- ✓ Always keep hands visible

201

Hands Up!

- ✓ Make a mental note of location
- ✓ Do not act aggressive or fight with law enforcement
- ✓ Do not run
- ✓ Do not argue with police
- ✓ Don does not engage in movements
- ✓ If verbally or physically assaulted by police, become passive assertive to the assault
- ✓ Allow "stop and frisk"
- ✓ Report police misconduct immediately to police agency, law makers and mayor, governor or Attorney General

What should I Not to do when a traffic stop is legitimate?
- ✓ Speed away from the scene
- ✓ Become aggressive at the scene
- ✓ Call the officer names and make threats
- ✓ Open car door and exit vehicle
- ✓ Don't allow passengers to get fussy with officers
- ✓ Don't argue about the incident
- ✓ Listen to the reasons why you were stopped
- ✓ Don't tell the officers you hate them
- ✓ Turn your music down until the stop is complete
- ✓ Keep smoking if officer request you to put out cigarettes
- ✓ Talk too much
- ✓ Move your hands all over the vehicle as if you are searching for something
- ✓ Refuse to shut off your engine

Hands Up!

- ✓ Call friends and family members to the scene, unless directed to do so by police
- ✓ Allow officers consent to search vehicle
- ✓ Unlock your doors in a dark space or neighborhood
- ✓ restart your engine without getting the okay from officers
- ✓ Allow passengers to be your elected spoke's person, unless he or she is an attorney
- ✓ Throw things out of the window
- ✓ Lean your seat back as the officers leave your window
- ✓ Check your console or glove box unless asked to do so
- ✓ Make sudden or quick movement in the vehicle, even if you are asked to retrieve something from the inside of the vehicle.

Recommendations
Racial bias, class discrimination, social-economic bigotry within police agencies; as well as racial animosity by citizens must be curbed or eliminated from the attitude and behavior to engage in authentic cultural or, intercultural and unbiased communication. There are officers and citizens who exercise bad judgment when confronted by hostility or non-hostile actions. Actions regarding racial or class motivated police practices or racial motivated set-ups to harm law enforcement officers can bring about deadly consequences or cause serious harm to an already fragile criminal justice system and community/police

Hands Up!

relationships. Thus, the recommendations listed are just to the tip of the iceberg educate, inform and train.
Citizens.

1. Learn the history of racial segregation and how police supported it due to laws in place.
2. If stopped by police, allow the police to carry out conversation to here if he or she is openly biased or racially prejudice against minorities.
3. Try to remember what was said and the time while complying with ONLY lawful orders.
4. If the officers are openly biased or racially prejudice, ask for their badge numbers.
5. If officers go back to their care in lieu of writing tickets, please turn on your recording device.
6. Do not try to record officers prior to conversations during the **Police**

RECOMMENDATIONS

POLICE

Upon considering the complexity of the entire relationship throughout the United States by education, information, training and experience, as well as reading journals, it is conclusive that Community/Police Relations works.

The ideology that we can afford to continue using Police/community Relations on certain groups and Community/Police Relations on another group is bias and will end in upscale violence amongst subcultures; and resistance against patrolling cops will increase as well.

The violence against police will fall sharply if we begin to teach Community/Policing as a Model Technological approach to today's citizens. For example, the Water Crisis in Flint, Michigan is widely known to have lead

Hands Up!

poisoning within the water pipes after switching over to city water in April 2014.

Research has shown that lead and its correlation to violence and violent crimes are linked together. found that lead exposure affects kids in communities across the country — not just in high-profile cities like Flint, Michigan.

According to Jennifer Doleac, of Reuters "this is worrisome, because elevated blood lead levels in kids have been linked to an array of developmental delays and behavioral problems. More ominously, this could also increase crime. Kevin Drum and others have argued that lead exposure caused the high crime rates during the 1980s and early 1990s.

There has been suggestive evidence of such a link for decades, though it hasn't gained much traction in research or policy circles. But the case that lead exposure causes crime recently became much stronger.

Author

206
Hands Up!

Lead exposure at young ages leaves children with problems like learning disabilities, ADHD, and impulse control problems; and (2) those problems cause them to commit crime as adults — particularly violent crime.

For many years, the major source of lead in the environment was leaded gasoline: car exhaust left lead behind to settle into dust on the roads and nearby land. When lead was removed from gasoline, lead levels in the environment fell, and kids avoided the lead exposure that caused these developmental problems. About 20 years later, when those kids became young adults, crime rates fell. This, proponents say, is what explains the mysterious and persistent decline in crime beginning in the early 1990s. Yet, in 2014, the need to save money caused the city leaders to create a lead poisoning issue as a model.

It's an intriguing idea — particularly since we don't have a better explanation for the big changes in crime rates during this period.

Several studies have found correlations between lead exposure and crime, at varying levels of geography (from neighborhoods to nations). But correlation, as we all know by now, does not imply causation. The causation of lead in correlation with violence may not be available now, but the people who committed the atrocities were let off the hook by Democratic State Government although the Republican State Government were the party that initiated the crimes. In years to come and even now, Flint is witnessing atrocities like their mom, friend, family member or community neighbor die of cancer, et.al caused by lead poisoning. But the crimes are going to skyrocket as those children with lead will become criminals. Thus, fix the lead atrocities to help police.

Chapter 19
COURTS

Upon examination of the Federal, Circuit, and District Courts, a wide opinion could not be reached because many Courts Rule by the Laws and case precedents already ruled on within the United States.

However, based on education, information, training and experience in Federal, Circuit and District Court within the 5th Circuit has caused an unsettling memory. The story was expressed in the chapter on Courts as the Judge appointed in that case have no reason for being on the Judicial Bench. When Judges reduce the chance of a fair trial by suppression of evidence; biased rulings, disrespect to the Defendant(s), expressed institutional racism from the Bench by ordering everyone to speak English, if they already do not. **"This is America!"** the Judge replied. Many Canons were abused/and disregarded as she used her judicial powers.

In early chapters, Cultural, Interpersonal, and Cross-Cultural Intelligence was written to advise the Criminal Justice System that CQ can adjust the way Judges speak to citizens entering the Courts. Cultural Intelligence is a Quan drum that if learned it will instill a new way of communicating with people who do not look or act like your racial or ethnic group.

The Courts is great in the U.S., but it is those Judicial Officials that are bigots or incompetent; or seeking to gain access to Convict Leasing that will assist them in becoming wealthy over time.

It is a shame that convict leasing, which started in the 40"s and continues will be the death of American Courts if we are NOT smart enough to elect or appoint legal scholars and those who understand cultural intelligence as well as intercultural relations.

Chapter 20

CORRECTIONS

In the past years up to 2019, Prison Reform has been an initiative that each U.S. President undertakes. PREA Data-Collection Activities, 2019 by Jessica Stroop, Shannan Catalano, Ph.D., *BJS Statisticians.*

On June 27, 2019 NCJ 252833 Describes activities during 2018 and 2019 by the Bureau of Justice Statistics to collect data and report on the incidence and effects of prison rape, as required by the Prison Rape Elimination Act of 2003

Hands Up!

(PREA; P.L. 108-79). This report describes the data collections and developmental activities during 2018 and 2019, particularly BJS's use of the National Survey of Youth in Custody. National Inmate Survey of Sexual Victimization to collect multiple incidences and prevalence of rape and assaults.

Correctional facilities may not measure the appropriate samples to correct unbiased decisions in sentencing for placement. The report meets the PREA requirement to report on BJS's activities for the preceding calendar year by June 30 of each year the Court Officer who offer punitive or sentencing for crimes committed ought to remain unbiased in all decisions. They are ordered by Canons to respect and uphold the dignity of the Courts.

In doing so, many Judges over time have made mistakes or intentionally went over the guidelines to sentence convicts; mainly drug dealers as the 90's under the Clintons brought the (3) Strike and out program that sentence the majority of Blacks to Prison as they were probably invested in the

Convict leasing Program. Prison Reform has brought the State of California to eliminate the 3-strikes and off to prison law by the Clintons.

Prison reform is one remedy to the ineffectiveness of our justice system that many states and the federal government have explored. Prison reform is focused on ensuring public safety and restoration for those impacted by crime through the creation of a constructive culture within our prison system.

These reforms seek to alter the circumstances of incarceration in ways that allow the system to model and incentivize the attitudes, behaviors, and lifestyles conducive to personal responsibility and self-control. Achieving these goals through prison reform usually falls within two broad categories.

First, ensuring access to programs which help individuals gain knowledge, skills, job training, and positive values during their period of incarceration and second, by revising correctional policies relationships. By providing individuals

Hands Up!

with opportunities to gain productive skills and equipping them to strengthen their positive relationships, we can help them achieve their full potential and transform their lives upon returning to our communities. Prison Reform was needed as some Racial Minorities who did not have education; access to training or jobs and without parents joined local gangs for protection. Soon gangs in California – infamous Crips/Bloods/64 and now 6/9 tray is on trial in a RICCO.

The indictments are related to homicides, racketeering by forcing stars to pay for protection; and many racial minorities or Blacks find themselves in the middle of a chaos. The sentencing of Black Rappers and White Rappers by using their music and following the money deposited in bank accounts for protection and recognition is taken seriously.

Upon conviction, many inmates use their hands to learn crafts or develop a business as Reform allows the inmates convicted to get an education, learn trades, but most of all, learn how not to return to the facilities. Programs that benefit the

Hands Up!

Prison Industrial Complex is "convict leasing program" being exposed as a good thing and not a bad immoral opportunist. The program would allow the Prisoner to work for less wages than others in the corporation or factory; and learn how to retain employment because he or she returns to the prison under guard and work Monday – Friday.

The negative stereo-type and possibly accurate to say that some elected and unelected officials would abuse the program by becoming a Correction Facility owner(s) and strike a deal with Judges and Prosecutors as well as Police Commissioners, Sheriffs or Chiefs of Police or (Designee) to cooperate. Cooperation include arresting, prosecuting, and ensuring long sentences as the Bureau of Prisons & Private prisons collaborate on how to increase wealth without knowledge of the truth.

The corruption can easily start as campaign donations or contributions for sentencing a person to Life in Prison for 50 grams of Powder

Hands Up!

Cocaine. Other people use Crack Cocaine or sell Crack and when caught, they may spend Double Life while involving authorities who can punish swiftly will destroy the people and their way of life.

The corruption is a secret society that determines the population and criminal records of citizens. However, corporate concerns are not our worry. What we can and should do is demand that CCA and the Federal and State Government politicians learn to value all lives, and NOT a few.
Criminal Justice Reform on all levels as we make all accountable for reforming a large portion of criminal justice. Facilities are becoming private and away from Public Prisons as it stifles union leaders. The primary reason is overspending money. Public Prisons are not only staffed with unions; but their desire to increase wages and fringe benefits while threatening NOT to do their jobs is another reason why Private Prisons are being built. Saving money – but getting Wealthy from Convict Leasing in some prisons.

Hands Up!

Conservatives and liberals are on the same side when it comes to money and private prisons. Private Prisons do not seem like a threat, but they are threats because there is no real oversight. If someone who is a Billionaire approach a Senator, Sheriff, Chief Judge or Prosecutor each 350,000 to vote for Private Prisons to be built creating good jobs. As years pass, many people who commit felonies involving racketeering are subjected various crimes according to new laws of BOP. However, a COPORATE RICCO was established because the money to incarcerate criminals and give them significant time or continue postponement of Judicial Hearings keeps people locked up have benefits; but could be criminal.

What if the more the person and groups of people remain incarcerated, every month or quarterly – money is sent to Prison owners? Would it be fair if the crime is murder? Each person locked down and waiting for Court dates on Rikers Island; Attica; Genesee County Jail; Jackson Prison 2002 Cooper St – Jackson MI are creating billions of

Hands Up!

dollars by profiting from penalties causing some or masses to go to Prison. Powerful people and wealthy private prison owners are profiting from the immigration fight.

In the meantime, many of the Correctional Officers on the take as drugs or contraband are transported into the private prisons are increasing. By allowing contraband to enter the Private Prisons, inmates can keep their minds off their next Court Date(s).

In some cases, some people in New York's Rikers Island – many young people and adults have been locked up for years after a traffic stop. Each inmate is possibly worth $300,000 Dollars. Thus, the Criminal Justice System that need reformation now is only a cash cow machine that most people have no idea about ideas and rights until books like Hand Up America "Community/Police Relations" hit the shelf. Community/Police Relations is a concept or idea of how to de-escalate conflict by using verbal Judo.

The judo being practiced or exercised is allowing the person needing help find tools.

What to do when you are locked up on warrants or fresh charges?

- ❖ Pray and Get to know the Savior
- ❖ Do not commit crimes, first!
- ❖ Write or call someone who knows what to do regarding your case if you are locked up.
- ❖ Never talk about your case with other inmates
- ❖ Never talk about your case with C.O.'s
- ❖ Never discuss anything of serious nature with any inmate.
- ❖ Report C.O's after they assault you
- ❖ Contact an Attorney
- ❖ Listen to your lawyer if they are not plea you out.
- ❖ Read everything that you get before you sign it.
- ❖ Never accept responsibility if you are innocent! Even if you are promised something.
- ❖ Avoid confrontations with C.0.'s or Inmates
- ❖ Avoid finding trouble to extend your time

Hands Up!

- ❖ Read the law books about your case law
- ❖ Write often to people who can help
- ❖ Do not listen to know one who wants to advise you on your case while inside.
- ❖ Write a letter to the prosecutor, if you know any thing that can help your case if you do not have an attorney.
- ❖ Write letters to politicians
- ❖ Write letters to the Officer that wrote the Report and acquired the Affidavit for Arrest.

What shouldn't I do while in prison?

- ❖ First, stay away from gangs and criminals outside of prisons
- ❖ Read for Hope Everyday
- ❖ Never disrespect the C.O.'s
- ❖ Never disrespect your attorney
- ❖ Never give others your money
- ❖ Always look to stay alone and to yourself
- ❖ Don't allow people to frequent your cell
- ❖ Don't become part of gangs
- ❖ Exercise on the yard
- ❖ Stay away from drugs
- ❖ Get an Education

Hands Up!

- Be persistent about why you are there
- Never take another person's charge
- See if a Law book can be purchased and brought inside of the prisons for studying
- Stay away from Drugs
- Use the Fruit of the Spirt (Gal. 5) NIV
- Pray Often
- Put other down and not lift them up
- Lift up Self
- Never put yourself down
- Try not to be with friends who commit crimes
- Work on CJ Reform with the world
- Help others and they will help you
- Learn about CJ Reform
- Learn about Prison Reform
- When you get out, if you live in a state, apply for a pardon.

Chapter 21

220
Hands Up!

Glossary Terms

Assault: make a physical attack on with force; verbally or an attempt to assault.

Battery: A willful touching of the person or another by the aggressor.

Choke Hold: a tight grip around a person's neck, used to restrain them by restricting their breathing.

Deadly Force: A use of force continuum or force that cause death by force.

Unlawful Arrest: An arrest or unusual detention without probable cause or reasonable suspicion.

Unlawful Conduct: Misconduct in Office or by Civilian unlawfully planning to hurt public servants or by police officers.

Unlawful Confession: A confession illegally extracted; usually by force by interview or interrogation.

Unlawful Search: An unlawful search conducted without a warrant or warrantless search without probable cause or reasonable suspicion.

Unlawful Seizure: An unlawful seizure usually comes after a unlawful search or warrantless search without probable cause or reasonable suspicion.

Immoral Purpose: An immoral person(s) who is apprehended performing immoral acts like prostitution in an alley or car.

Imprison: A place or persons incarcerated or behind prison walls due to being convicted of crimes.

Indecent Exposure: Offensive Act that includes pants handing off one's waist called Saggy Pants.

Infractions: Rules violations such as traffic fines or disobeying stop sighs or traffic signals etc.

Internal Affairs: An Internal Division of Law Enforcement whose duty is to investigate sheriffs or police officers who violate rules or laws.

Interrogation: A technique used by police investigators to extract vital information to prove or eliminate suspects of a crime.

Intimidating: The intent to frighten a person or people or subculture to gain momentum for the purpose.

Involuntary Manslaughter: A death of human beings without lawful justifications.

Kidnapping: Any armed or unarmed person who deliberately takes away a child, minor or adult with intent to hide from family or friends is engaging in kidnapping.

Legal Search: A search conducted by authorization from the owner of the property; or warrantless search such as a traffic stop with drugs seen with the naked eye**; or with a search warrant.**

Lethal/Non-Lethal Force: In the force continuum policy, non-lethal force is applied when a baton or pepper spray is used.

Vicarious Liability: Vicarious liability is when a person or department allows a ride alone and the ride alone use his gun to kill a man engaged in a misdemeanor.

Loitering: A person or people who usually frequent stores or commercial land without the owner's permission.

Manslaughter: The willful killing of a person without premeditation and without excuse.

Minor Offense: Usually a minor offense is a judgement call that may involve graffiti.

Misdemeanor: Violations of a crime that can net imprisonment from 1-year & 1 day. A misdemeanor can transpire from an unpaid traffic citation and/or committing a crime that does not meet the sentencing guidelines of imprisonment of more than 1-year & 1 day.

Homicide: A willful murder or deliberate killing with premeditation (intent) & (planning) the crime(s) that result in the loss of life of people or person.

Negligent Homicide: Any person or persons who accidently commits a crime that result in negligence. Negligent Homicide can occur or is applicable in Drunk Driving Cases where the Victim dies in the car or as a pedestrian without deliberate intent or motive.

Nuisance Crimes: Nuisance Crimes are usually crimes that children may engage in such as skipping school (status offense); or graffiti; or loud noise from cars (music) etc.

Operating While Impaired (OWI): The charge OWI occurs when a person who consumes alcohol beverages and their Blood Alcohol Content (B.A.C) of .10 or more.

Police Brutality: Police Brutality is usually initiated by the police/sheriffs as they intentionally use their position of power by becoming the Prosecutor and Judge and Correction Officer on the streets prior to the arrest. In some cases, arrest are NOT effected because brutality was relieving for the officer.

Probable Cause: Probable Cause is when near certainty that surpass reasonable suspicion to effect an arrest or the prosecutor complete an Affidavit of Probable Cause for arrest of persons of interest.

Racial Profiling: Racial Profiling occurs when the authority selects a subculture or race of people different from their racial identity to exercise the power provided to the person in charge due to the other person's racial make-up.

Resisting Arrest: When law enforcement is summoned by 911 Dispatcher and the person who called identifies the suspect of a new crime seeks to run or wrestle with police to ascertain freedom from custody is resisting arrest. Resisting arrest can occur after an officer Verbally Orders the suspect to surrender.

Subpoena: An order usually by a Court Officer such as a Judge or Prosecutor having a subpoena is an order. But if the order is NOT signed by a Judge Compelling interested parties to appear as a witness or suspect to testify against another or self can be avoided by NOT accepting the Subpoena out of the Court Officer's sight.

Suspect: A person of interest that is wanted for questioning of crime(s) or matter related to misdemeanor and felonies.

Direct Testimony: Direct testimony is when the plaintiff or defendant or witnesses provide direct testimony of what occurred.

Indirect Testimony: Indirect Testimony **can be used to support the direct testimony.**

Undercover Sting: An undercover sting is when law enforcement set up a physical or virtual presence to use subterfuge such as acting like or sounding like a teenager talking to a man who is 4 times her age seeking sex from an underage child who is the law enforcement officer acting in her stead.

Undercover stings are primarily used on drug interdiction programs and cybercrimes involving underage children being solicited for sex by phone or computer. The perp usually requests lewed (naked) pictures
The purpose is to control and manipulate the child into trusting them and then they take full advantage.

Unjustified Shooting: Unjustified shootings can be from a civilian in the wrong or office under the Color of Law that engage in unjustified shootings **or deadly force** "Choke Hold".

Verbal Abuse: Abuse is associated with family or friends and even a intimate spouse or person. But a person seeking to develop the community will not abuse people or the Community/Police Officer helping them. Never abuse the officers.

Verbal Permission: Verbal Permission expressed to give consent to law enforcement to enter their home to look around or limited search; or the verbal permission is usually given is on traffic stops. A civilian who ran the traffic signal or forgot to signal when changing lanes can be stopped.

But it is when you authorize another person who can change your life overnight by verbal consent.

Victim: A person who is assaulted or battered (Domestic) or Non-Domestic is a victim. A victim is the complainant or allege plaintiff in case law. A victim can be someone who has lost everything due to FRAUD or Identity Theft.

Ward of the Court: A person that is subject to Court Authority as a delinquent under the age of 17 can become a Ward of the Court if the parents are unfit to engage in parental responsibilities.

Warrantless Search: A search & seizure of information or contraband can be ascertained in a warrantless search.

Judges sign off on warrants. But Warrantless Searches does NOT need a Court Officer signature. Warrantless Searches can immediately thwart terrorism or stop an egregious act of harm on domestic soil.

Operating While Impaired (OWI) on a motorized vehicle.

Witness: A Witness is an individual that directly observed or indirectly associated with a Civil or Criminal Law. The purpose of the witness is to support or defend the Plaintiff or Defendant Civil or Criminal allegations.

Witness Protection: Witness Protection Program is usually used by Federal Prosecutors with the consent of Judges to place a Witness i.e. (Mafia) Witness and other gang related witnesses that are usually charged with Racketeering.

Witness Tampering: Any person who influence by threat; hurt, harm or compelling a witness be dishonest for fear of danger.

Reference

Branham, Lynn S. 2002. *The Law of Sentencing, Corrections, and Prisoners' Rights in a Nutshell.* 6th ed. St. Paul, Minn.: West Group. Oliss, Philip. 1995. "Mandatory

CBS. (2019). NYPD Officer Dies from an Apparent Self-Inflicted Gunshot Wound in 9th Officer Suicide of the Year. Retrieved from CBS www.cbsnews.com/news/nypd-officer-suicide-nypd-officer-dies-from-apparent-self-inflicted-gunshot-wound-

Gelko, Bob. (2019). Report slams the quiet way California judges are disciplined. Retrieved from http://www.sfgate.com/news/article/Report-slams-the-quiet-way-California-judges-are-7213677.php

Minimum Sentencing: Discretion, the Safety and the Sentencing. Guidelines." *University of Cincinnati Law Review* 63. Parson, Elizabeth A. 1994. "Shifting the Balance of Power: Prosecutorial Discretion Under the Federal Sentencing

Mostellar, J. (2019) Why Prison Reform Matter in America. Retrieved from https://www.charleskochinstitute.org/issue-areas/criminal-justice-policing-reform/why-prison-reform-matters/

Walker, T. (2019). Trump and Congress Take a "First Step" to Reduce Mass Incarceration. Retrieved at http://www.CJ reforms.

Reitz, Kevin R. 2002. "American Law Institute, Model Penal Code: Sentencing, Plan for Revision." *Buffalo Criminal Law Review* 6.

Spohn, Cassia C. 2002. *How Do Judges Decide: The Search for Fairness and Justice in Punishment?* Thousand Oaks, Calif.: Sage. The importance of criminal justice reform depends on everyone to examine the system of today and prevent injustices of tomorrow.

Author's Biography

David R. Dicks, Former Chief of Police of the most dangerous city in America known as Flint, Michigan. The Chief's style and approach to law enforcement is Community/Police Relations – which involve allowing the people within their own communities and neighborhoods to lead in challenging crime by becoming the Agency's eyes and ears.

Chief David R. Dicks received numerous awards and recognition after education information and training from the military to law enforcement officer. Chief David R Dicks profound training at the Homeland Security Management Institute in Rochester, NY. As a Deputy Chief Community Relations; Flint/Genesee Crime Stoppers as a Police Inspector, the Police Mini-Station were consumed by civilians. The community leaders and helpers assist on huge events:

Hands Up!

Marathons, Dignitary Protection, (Halloween Night) and the head of community debriefing with crime stats. Attended N.Y Homeland Security Training. The now retired and disabled public servant at heart cannot leave this book in his system of publications. He served onboard two Naval Ships: USS Fulton AS-11 (Submarine-Tender) Groton, CT; & USS Avenger MCM-1 (Mine Sweeper) with Acoustics in Charleston, SC. Naval Duties included working alongside NIS/NCIS in acting as an intelligence officer or confidential informant in developing information that exposed Drug Trafficking and Drug Interdiction.

An Honorable Discharge occurred on the emergency basis after multiple threats were aimed at Chief Dicks. David R. Dicks is the author of numerous books on law enforcement; psychology behind police suicides; physical, emotional, behavioral, and cognitive signs and symptoms of PTSD. This book is inspired by/for history as we change the **Criminal Justice System** using Hands Up America to begin the journey.

Education: Master Science Degree HSA 2015; MSA General Administration 2014; MSA Leadership; MSA HRA Certifications; 2016. **Central Michigan University. Michigan**

Bachelor of Arts in Human Resource Management, 2009: **Spring Arbor University, Michigan**

Associate of Science Degree: Criminal Justice Administration, Mott Community College, 2004

2012 Poverty Cops Film 1:36minutes based on Poverty Cops the Book (2007).

2008: Ordinance: Wrote City Teen Dancing Laws to Reduce Juvenile Crime

2006-2007: High School Graduation Commencement Speaker; Don't Take the Title; Take the Testimony"
2007 City Law School Instructor; City of

Flint, MI. Mayor Donald J. Williamson

2004-2005: Community/Police Relations Award/Recipient of the City of Flint
2006-2007: City's Law School Instructor

Publications:
2000-2005: First Line of Defense: 1st 2nd and

2007: Officer Down: "Death Before Dishonor 2012: Poverty Cops "Inner Darkness"

2012: Poverty Cops: "Inner Darkness" First Line of Defense Publishing, 2012 (FLD)

Hands Up America: (2020) "A Guide to Community/Police Relations. Publisher: Legacy Publishing, Orlando, Florida

www.ingramcontent.com/pod-product-compliance
Lightning Source LLC
Chambersburg PA
CBHW070327220526
45467CB00001B/56